For Engineers & Designers

DesignSpark Mechanical

200 3D PRACTICE DRAWINGS

SACHIDANAND JHA

cadin360°
Learning Tutorials

Dear Reader,

Thank you for choosing **DesignSpark Mechanical** book. This book is part of a family of premium-quality CADIN360 books, all of which are written by Outstanding author who combine practical experience with a gift for teaching.

CADIN360 was founded in 2016. More than 3 years later, we're still committed to producing consistently exceptional books. With each of our titles, we're working hard to set a new standard for the industry. From the paper we print on, to the authors we work with, our goal is to bring you the best books available.

I hope you see all that reflected in these pages. I'd be very interested to hear your comments and get your feedback on how we're doing. Feel free to let me know what you think about this or any other CADIN360 book by sending me an email at contactus@cadin360.com.

If you think you've found a technical error in this book, please visit https://cadin360.com/contact-us/.
Customer feedback is critical to our efforts at CADIN360.

Best regards,

Sachidanand Jha
Founder & CEO, CADIN360

DesignSpark Mechanical

Published by
CADIN360
cadin360.com
Copyright © 2019 by CADIN360, All rights reserved.

Limit of Liability/Disclaimer of Warranty:

The publisher and the author make no representations or warranties with respect to the accuracy or completeness of the contents of this work and specifically disclaim all warranties, including without limitation warranties of fitness for a particular purpose. No warranty may be created or extended by sales or promotional materials. The advice and strategies contained herein may not be suitable for every situation. This work is sold with the understanding that the publisher is not engaged in rendering legal, accounting, or other professional services. If professional assistance is required, the services of a competent professional person should be sought. Neither the publisher nor the author shall be liable for damages arising herefrom. The fact that an organization or Web site is referred to in this work as a citation and/or a potential source of further information does not mean that the author or the publisher endorses the information the organization or Web site may provide or recommendations it may make. Further, readers should be aware that Internet Web sites listed in this work may have changed or disappeared between when this work was written and when it is read.

Examination Copies

Books received as examination copies in any form such as paperback and eBook are for review only and may not be made available for the use of the student. These files may not be transferred to any other party. Resale of examination copies is prohibited

Electronic Files

The electronic file/eBook in any form of this book is licensed to the original user only and may not be transferred to any other party.

Disclaimer:

All trademarks and registered trademarks appearing in this book are the property of their respective owners.

Preface

DesignSpark Mechanical

❖ This book contain 200 CAD practice exercises and drawings.

❖ This book does not provide step by step tutorial to design 3D models.

❖ S.I Unit is used.

❖ Predominantly used Third Angle Projection.

❖ This book is for **DesignSpark Mechanical** and Other Feature-Based Modeling Software such as Inventor, SolidWorks, NX, Solid Edge, AutoCAD, PTC Creo etc.

❖ It is intended to provide Drafters, Designers and Engineers with enough 3D CAD exercises for practice on **DesignSpark Mechanical**.

❖ It includes almost all types of exercises that are necessary to provide, clear, concise and systematic information required on industrial machine part drawings.

❖ Third Angle Projection is intentionally used to familiarize Drafters, Designers and Engineers in Third Angle Projection to meet the expectation of world wide Engineering drawing print.

❖ Clear and well drafted drawing help easy understanding of the design.

❖ This book is for Beginner, Intermediate and Advance CAD users.

❖ These exercises are from Basics to Advance level.

❖ Each exercises can be assigned and designed separately.

❖ No Exercise is a prerequisite for another. All dimensions are in mm.

❖ Note: Assume any missing dimensions.

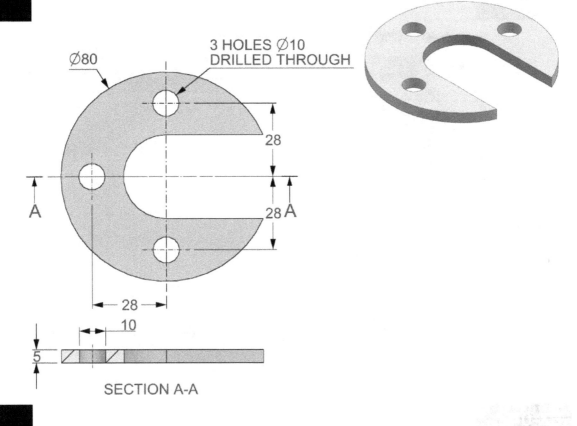

∅80

3 HOLES ∅10
DRILLED THROUGH

28

28 A

A

28

10

5

SECTION A-A

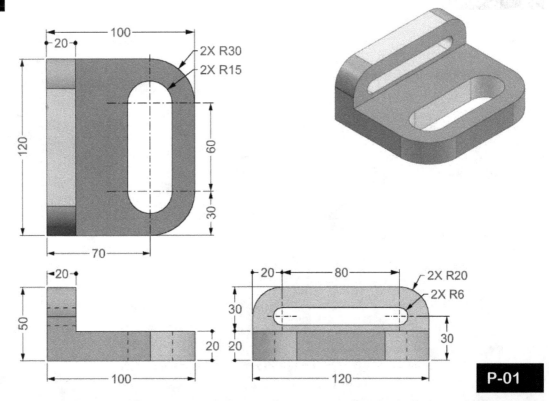

100

20

2X R30

2X R15

120

60

30

70

20

50

20

100

20

80

2X R20

2X R6

30

30

20

120

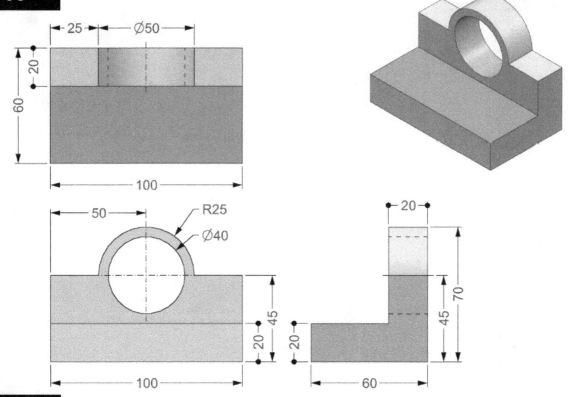

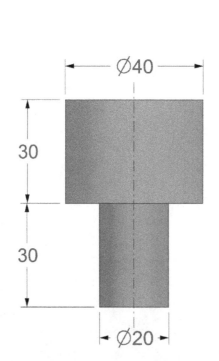

EX-05

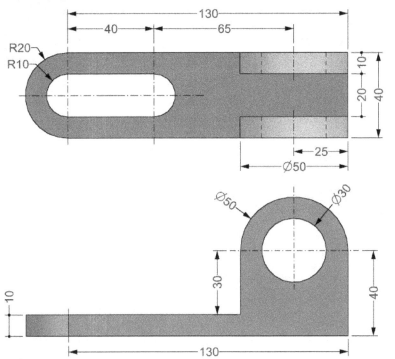

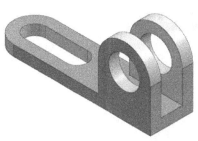

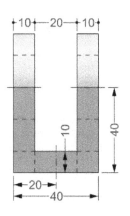

EX-06

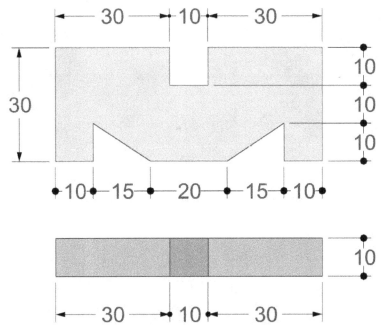

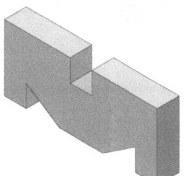

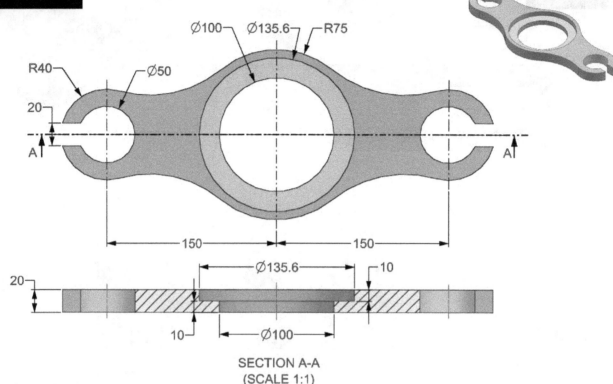

Ø100　Ø135.6　R75

R40　Ø50

20

A

A

150　150

Ø135.6　10

20

10　Ø100

SECTION A-A
(SCALE 1:1)

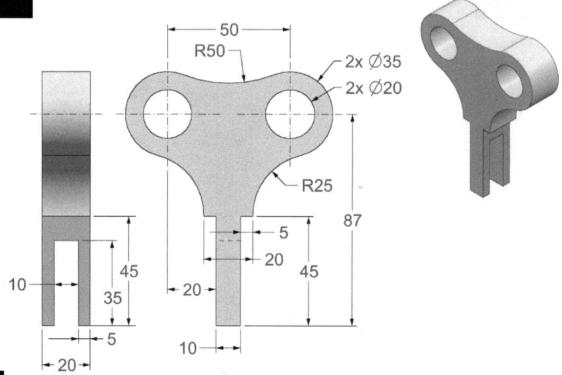

50

R50

2x Ø35

2x Ø20

R25

87

45

5

20

20

45

10

10

45

35

5

20

EX-09

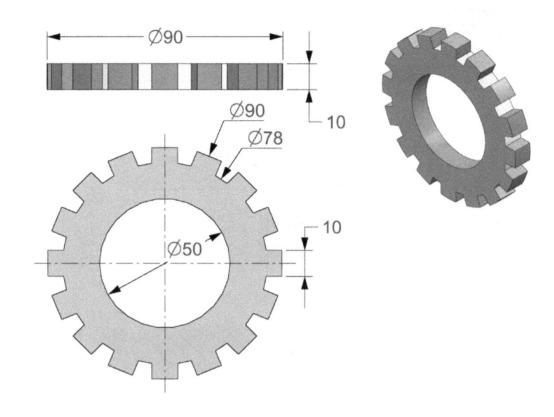

⌀90

10

⌀90
⌀78

⌀50

10

EX-10

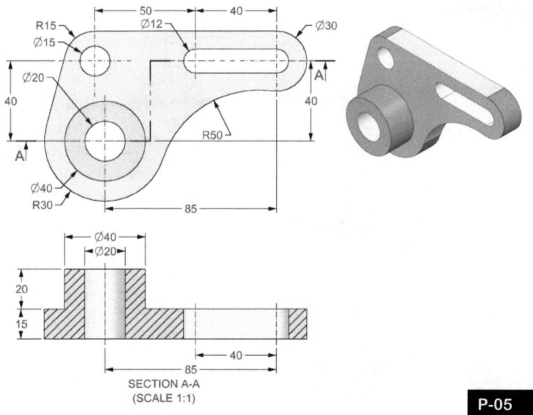

R15
⌀15
⌀20
⌀40
R30

50
⌀12
40
⌀30

40
40
R50
85

A
A

⌀40
⌀20

20
15

40
85

SECTION A-A
(SCALE 1:1)

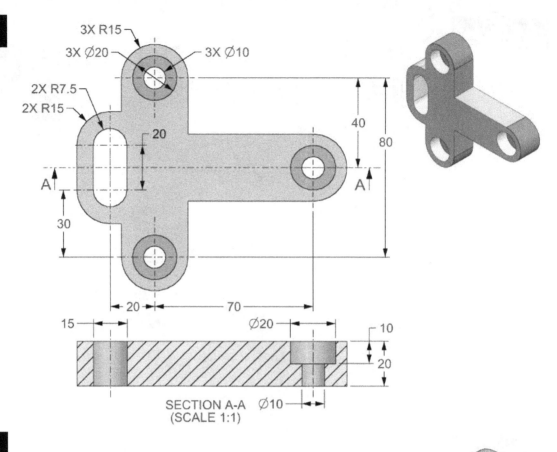

3X R15
3X Ø20
3X Ø10
2X R7.5
2X R15
40
80
20
A
30
A
20
70

15
Ø20
10
20

SECTION A-A
(SCALE 1:1)
Ø10

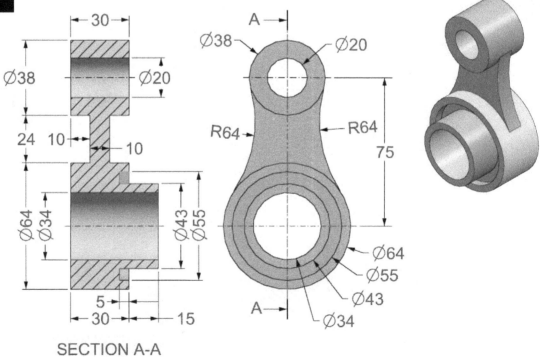

30
Ø38
Ø20
24 10
10
Ø64
Ø34
Ø43
Ø55
5
30
15

A
Ø38
Ø20
R64
R64
75
Ø64
Ø55
Ø43
Ø34
A

SECTION A-A
(SCALE 1:1)

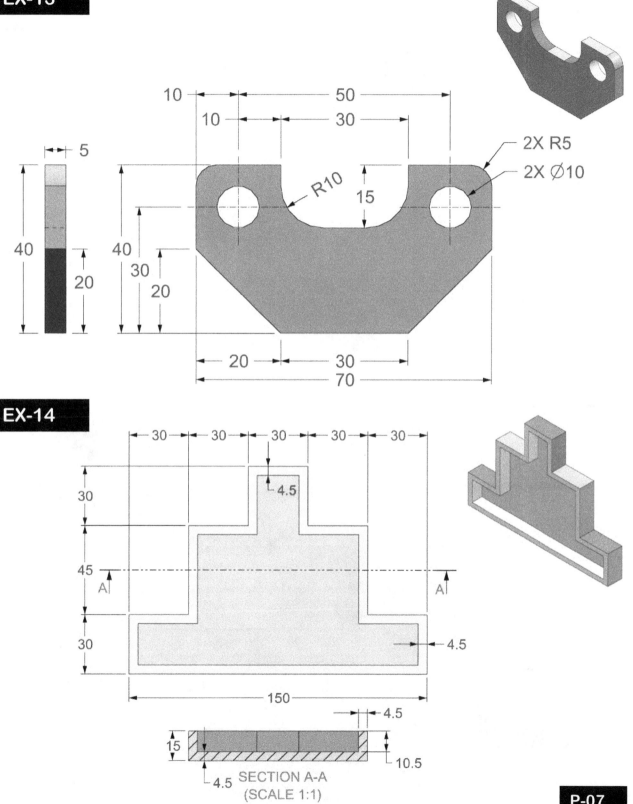

EX-13

10
10
50
30

2X R5
2X Ø10

5

R10

15

40
40
30
20
20

20
30
70

EX-14

30
30
30
30
30

30

4.5

45

A
A

30

4.5

150
4.5

15

4.5

10.5

SECTION A-A
(SCALE 1:1)

P-07

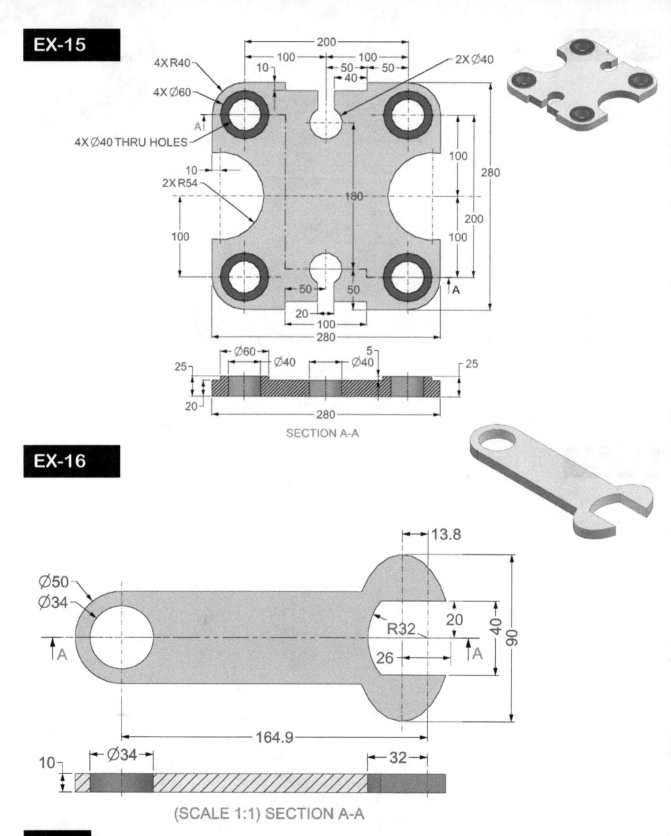

EX-15

4X R40
4X Ø60
4X Ø40 THRU HOLES
2X R54
2X Ø40

200
100
100
10
50
50
40
100
280
280
200
100
180
100
10
50
50
100
20
100
280

Ø60
Ø40
5
Ø40
25
25
20
280

SECTION A-A

EX-16

Ø50
Ø34
13.8
20
40
90
R32
26
164.9

A
A

10
Ø34
32

(SCALE 1:1) SECTION A-A

P-08

EX-17

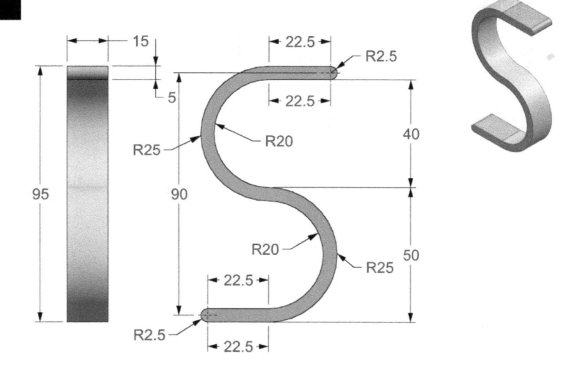

15
5
R2.5
22.5
22.5
R25
R20
40
95
90
R20
50
R25
22.5
R2.5
22.5

EX-18

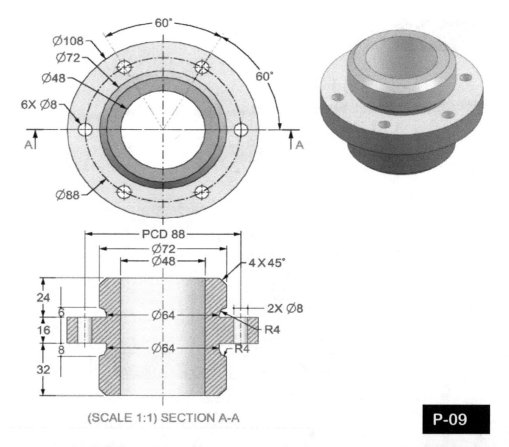

60°
Ø108
Ø72
60°
Ø48
6X Ø8
A
A
Ø88

PCD 88
Ø72
Ø48
4 X 45°
24
6
Ø64
2X Ø8
16
R4
8
Ø64
R4
32

(SCALE 1:1) SECTION A-A

P-09

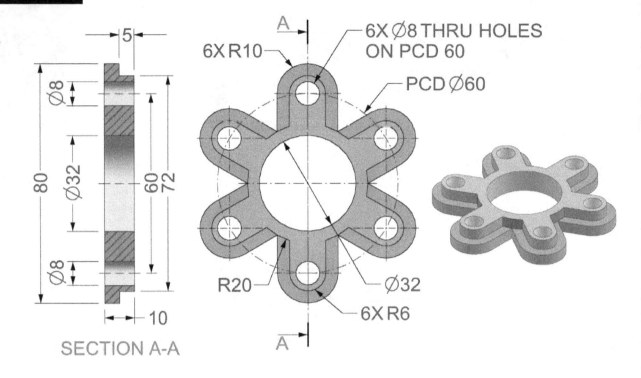

5

$\varnothing 8$

$\varnothing 32$

80

$\varnothing 8$

60

72

10

SECTION A-A

A

6X R10

6X $\varnothing 8$ THRU HOLES
ON PCD 60

PCD $\varnothing 60$

R20

$\varnothing 32$

6X R6

A

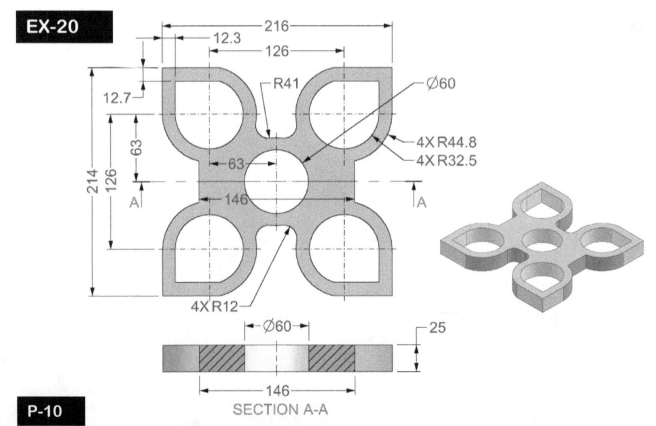

216

12.3

126

R41

$\varnothing 60$

12.7

63

214

126

63

4X R44.8

4X R32.5

A

146

A

4X R12

$\varnothing 60$

25

146

SECTION A-A

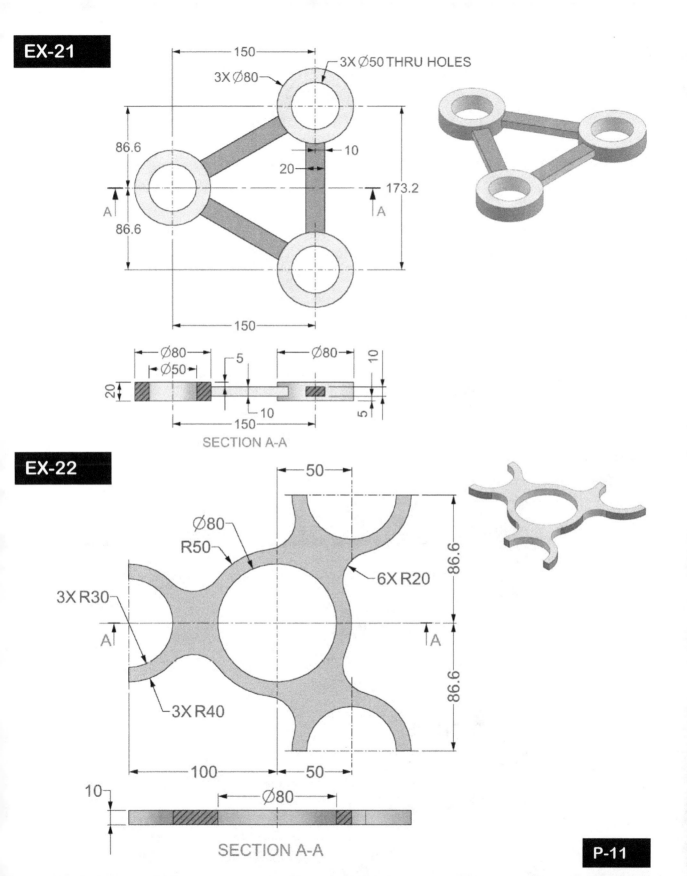

EX-21

150

3X Ø50 THRU HOLES

3X Ø80

86.6

10

20

173.2

A

86.6

A

150

Ø80   5   Ø80   10

Ø50

20   10   5

150

SECTION A-A

EX-22

50

Ø80

R50

86.6

6X R20

3X R30

A   A

3X R40

86.6

100   50

10

Ø80

SECTION A-A

P-11

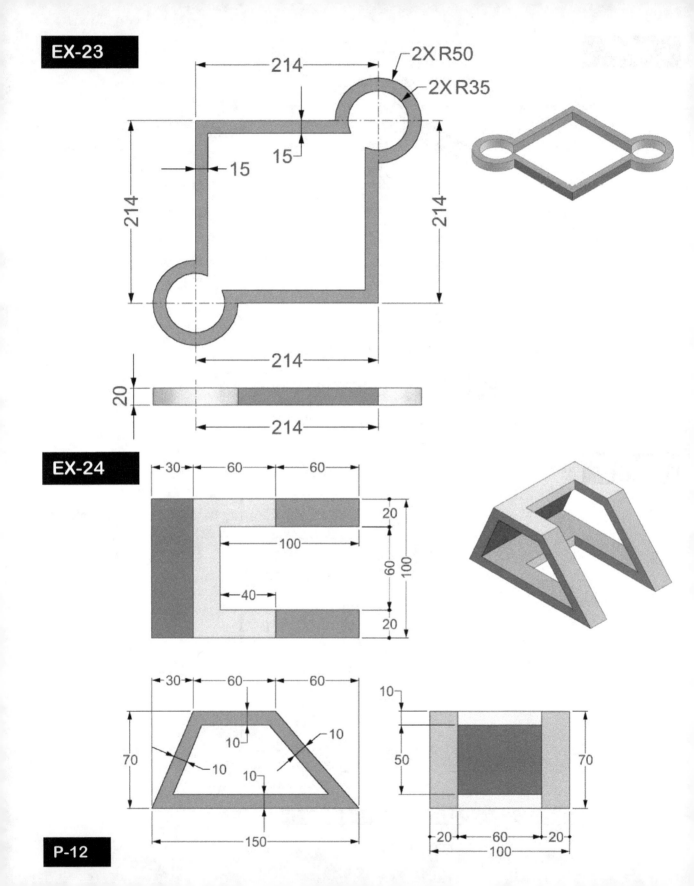

EX-23

2X R50
2X R35
214
15
15
214
214
214
214
20
214

EX-24

30 · 60 · 60
20
100
60 · 100
40
20

30 · 60 · 60
10
10
70
10
10
10
150

10
50
70
20 · 60 · 20
100

P-12

EX-25

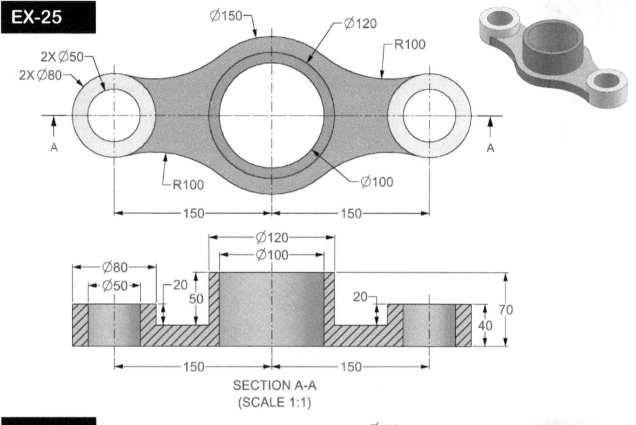

Ø150
Ø120
R100
2X Ø50
2X Ø80
R100
Ø100
150
150

SECTION A-A
(SCALE 1:1)

Ø80
Ø50
20
50
Ø120
Ø100
20
70
40
150
150

EX-26

Ø24
Ø44
Ø36

A   A

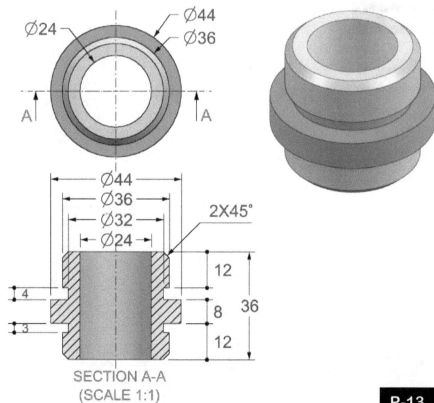

Ø44
Ø36
Ø32
Ø24
2X45°
12
36
8
12
4
3

SECTION A-A
(SCALE 1:1)

EX-27

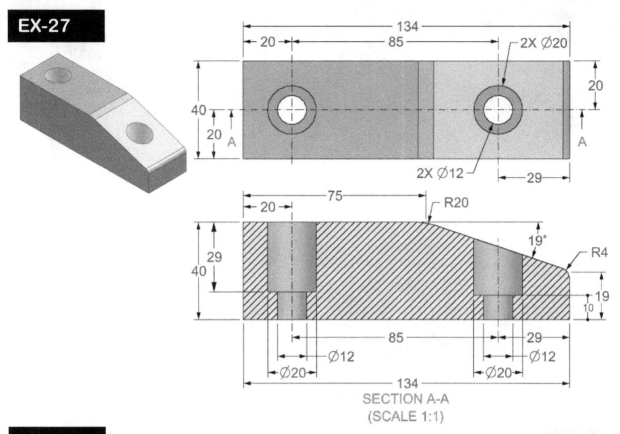

134
20
85
2X Ø20
20
40
20
A
A
2X Ø12
29

20
75
R20
19°
R4
29
40
19
10
Ø12
85
29
Ø12
Ø20
Ø20
134
SECTION A-A
(SCALE 1:1)

EX-28

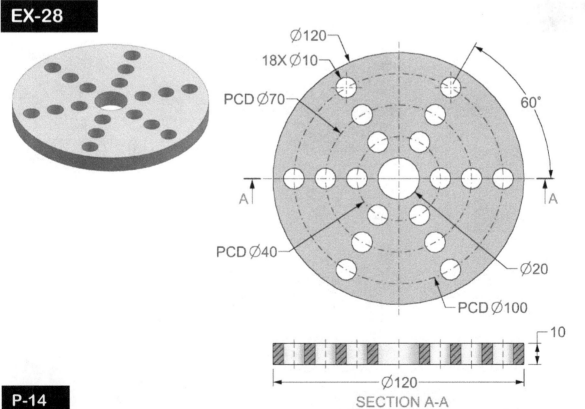

Ø120
18X Ø10
PCD Ø70
60°
PCD Ø40
Ø20
PCD Ø100
10
Ø120
SECTION A-A

EX-29

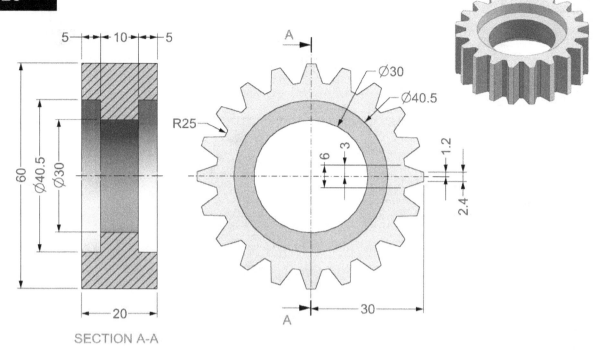

SECTION A-A

5 | 10 | 5

60
⌀40.5
⌀30

20

A

⌀30
⌀40.5
R25

6
3

1.2
2.4

30

EX-30

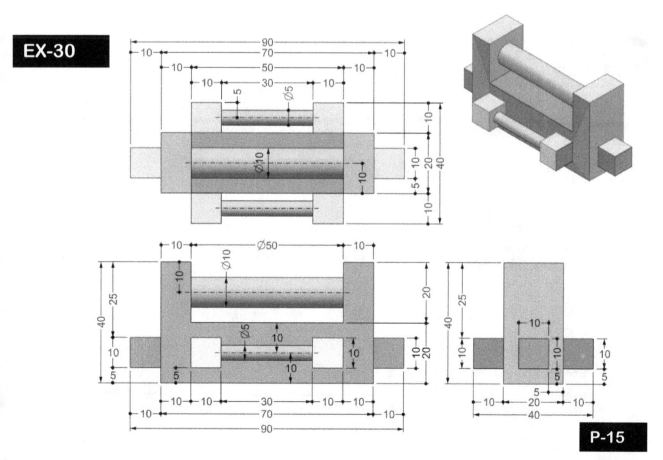

90
70
50
30
10
10
10
10
⌀5
5
10
⌀10
10
10
10
20
40
5
10

⌀50
⌀10
10
10
25
40
⌀5
10
10
10
5
10
10
30
10
10
70
10
90
20
20
10
20

40
25
10
5
10
10
5
5
10
20
10
40

P-15

EX-31

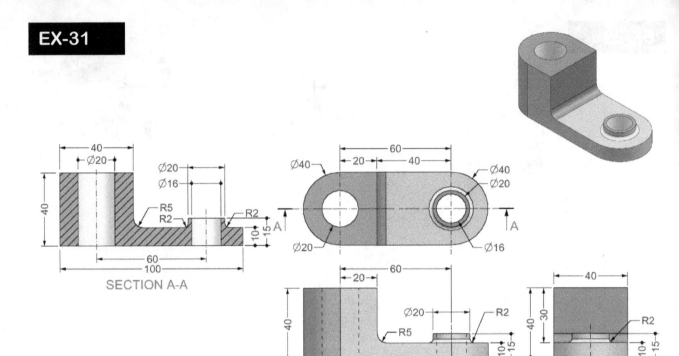

SECTION A-A

EX-32

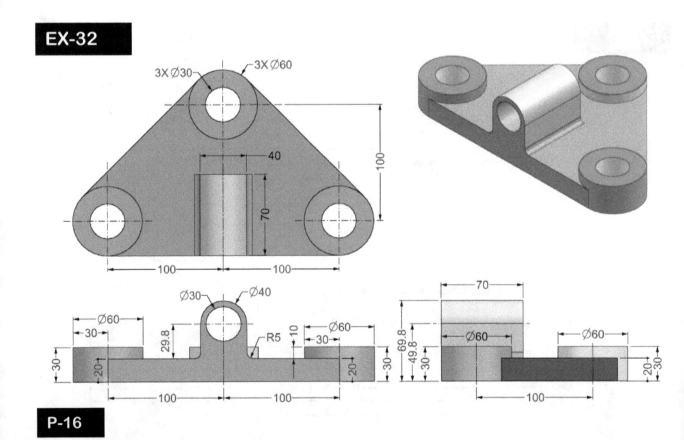

P-16

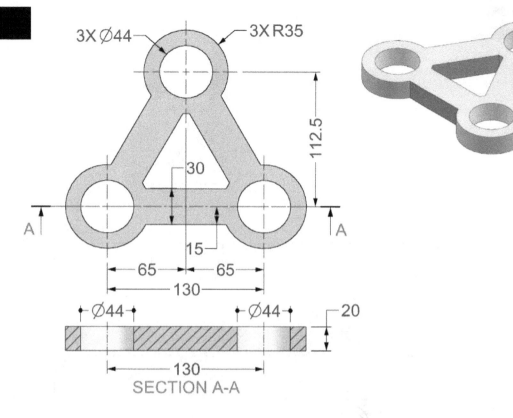

3X Ø44 — 3X R35

112.5

30

15

65 — 65

130

Ø44 — Ø44 — 20

130

SECTION A-A

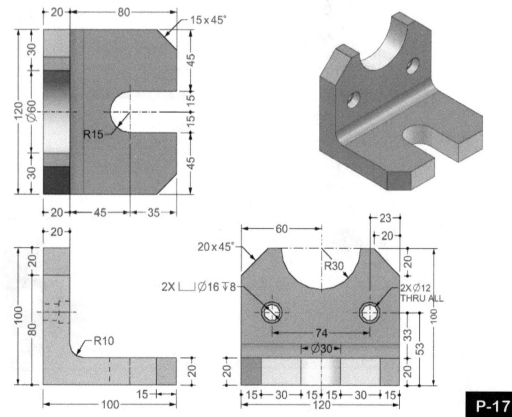

20 — 80 — 15 x 45°

30

45

120 — Ø60 — 15 15

R15 — 15

30 — 45

20 — 45 — 35

20

20

100 — 80

R10

15

100

23

20

60

20 x 45° — R30

2X ⌴ Ø16 ↧8 — 2X Ø12 THRU ALL

74 — 100

Ø30 — 33 — 53

20

15 — 30 — 15 15 — 30 — 15

120

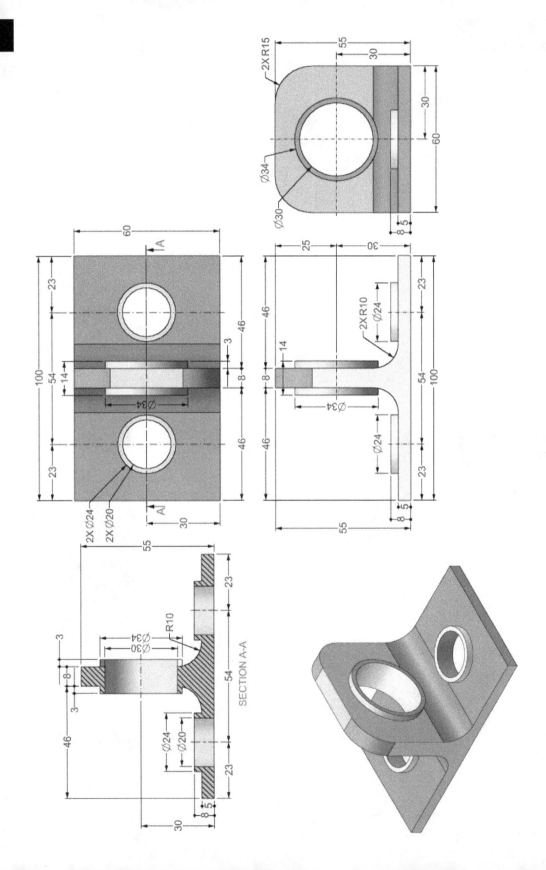

2X R15

55
30
30
60
Ø34
Ø30
8.5

60
23
46
3
8
54
14
Ø34
46
23
100
2X Ø24
2X Ø20
30
A
A

25
30
46
14
2X R10
Ø24
23
54
100
8
Ø34
Ø24
46
23
8.5
55

3
Ø34
Ø30
R10
8
3
Ø24
Ø20
46
55
23
54
23
8.5
30
SECTION A-A

EX-36

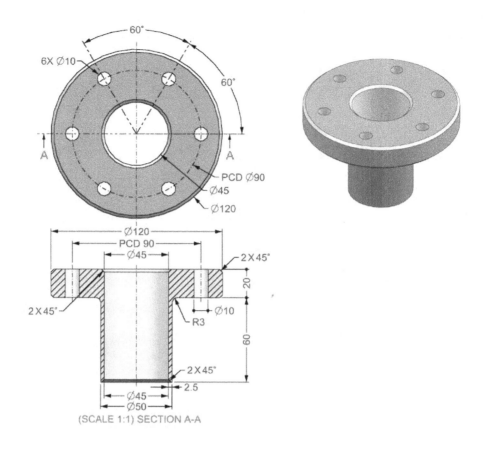

6X Ø10
60°
60°
PCD Ø90
Ø45
Ø120
A
A

Ø120
PCD 90
Ø45
2 X 45°
20
2 X 45°
Ø10
R3
60
2 X 45°
2.5
Ø45
Ø50

(SCALE 1:1) SECTION A-A

EX-37

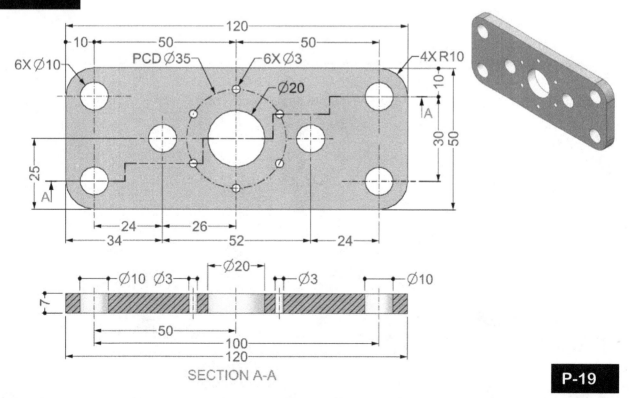

120
10
50
50
6X Ø10
PCD Ø35
6X Ø3
4X R10
Ø20
10
A
30
50
25
A
24
26
34
52
24

Ø20
Ø10 Ø3
Ø3
Ø10
7
50
100
120

SECTION A-A

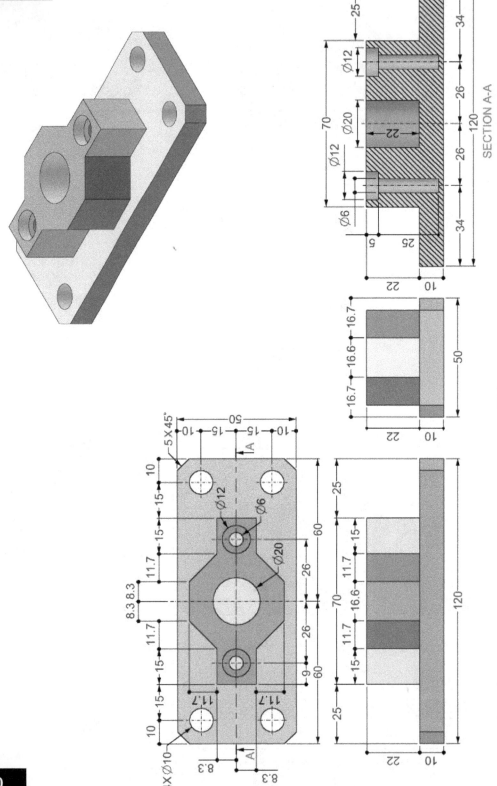

SECTION A-A

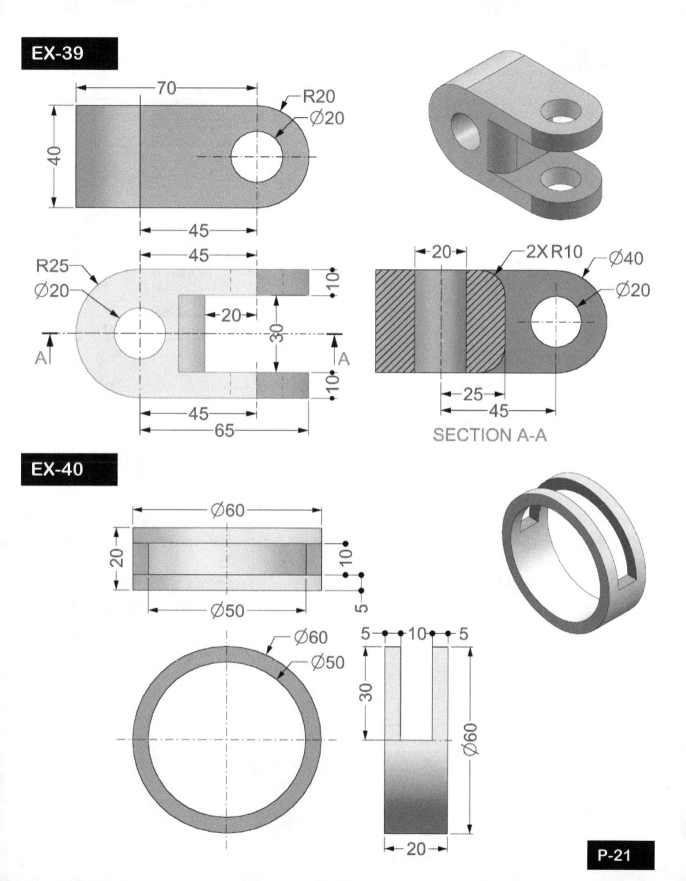

EX-39

70

R20
Ø20

40

45

45

R25
Ø20

20

30

A

A

45

65

10

10

20

2X R10

Ø40

Ø20

25

45

SECTION A-A

EX-40

Ø60

20

10

5

Ø50

Ø60

Ø50

5   10   5

30

Ø60

20

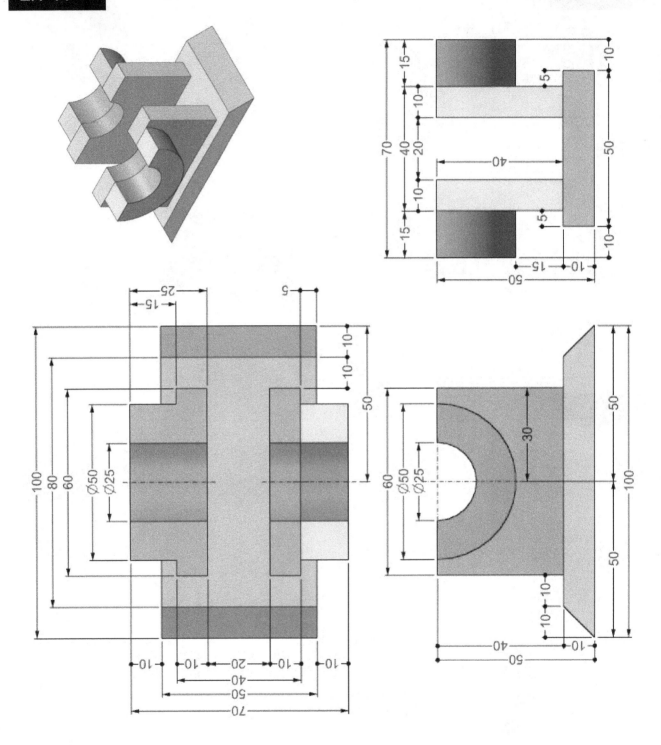

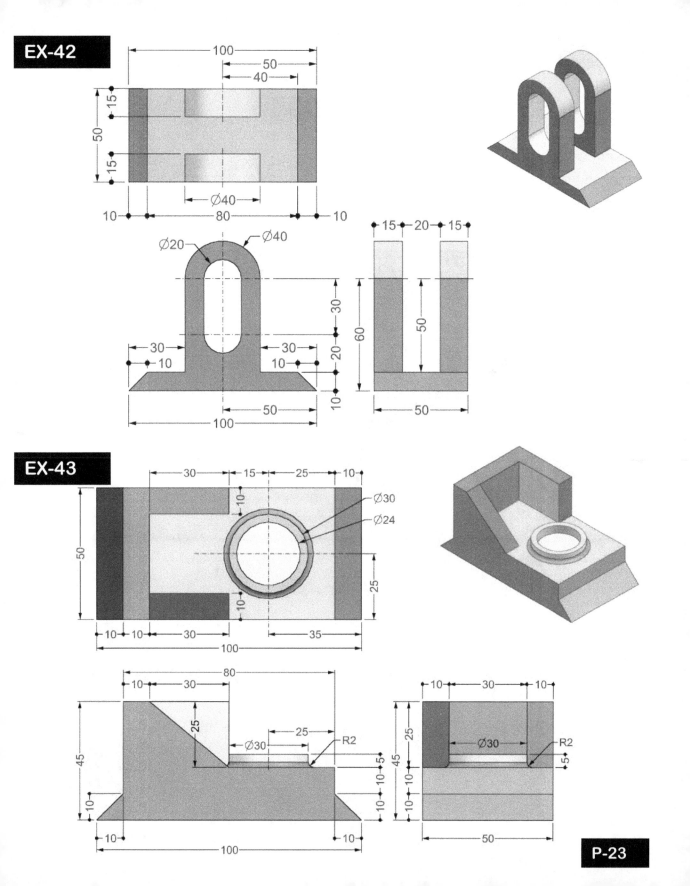

EX-42

EX-43

P-23

EX-44

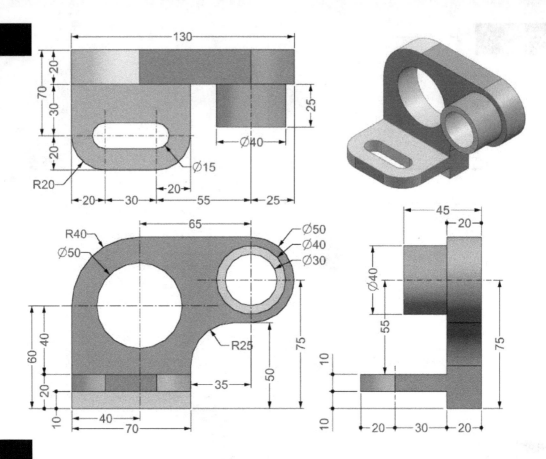

EX-45

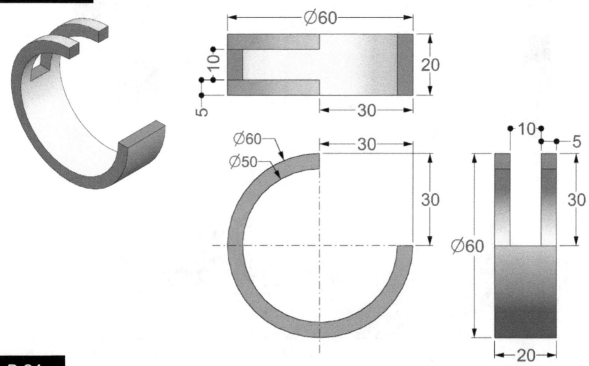

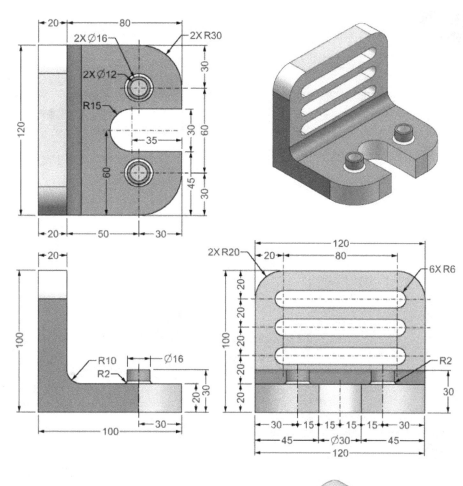

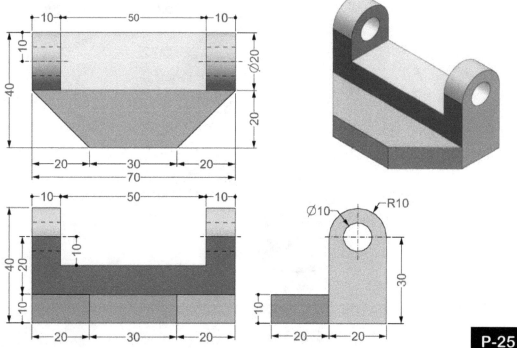

EX-48

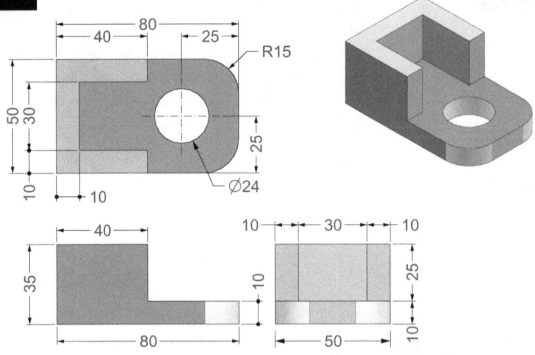

EX-49

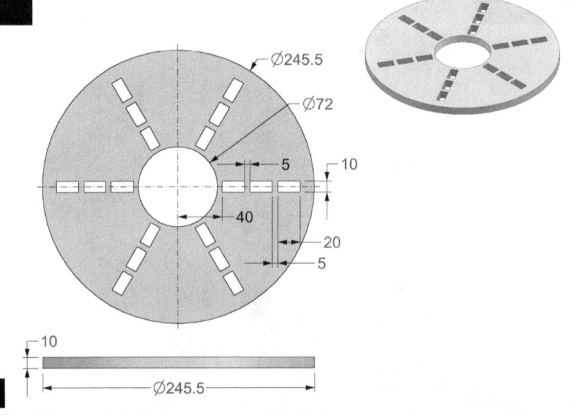

P-26

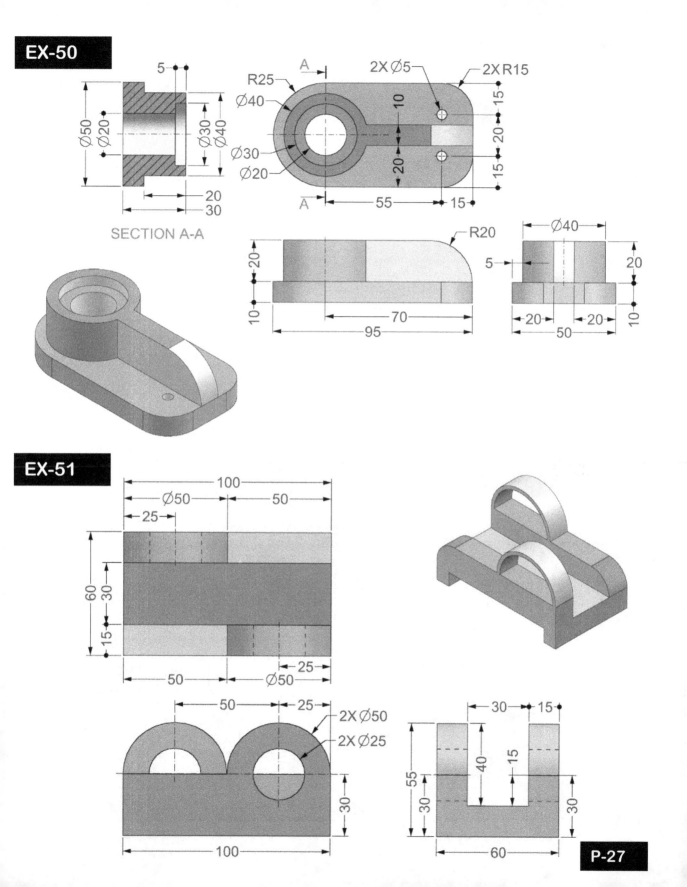

EX-50

5
Ø50
Ø20
Ø30
Ø40
20
30

SECTION A-A

A
R25
Ø40
Ø30
Ø20
2X Ø5
2X R15
10
20
15
20
15
55
15
A

R20
20
10
70
95

Ø40
5
20
20
20
50
10

EX-51

100
Ø50
50
25
60
30
15
50
25
Ø50

50
25
2X Ø50
2X Ø25
30
100

30
15
55
40
15
30
30
60

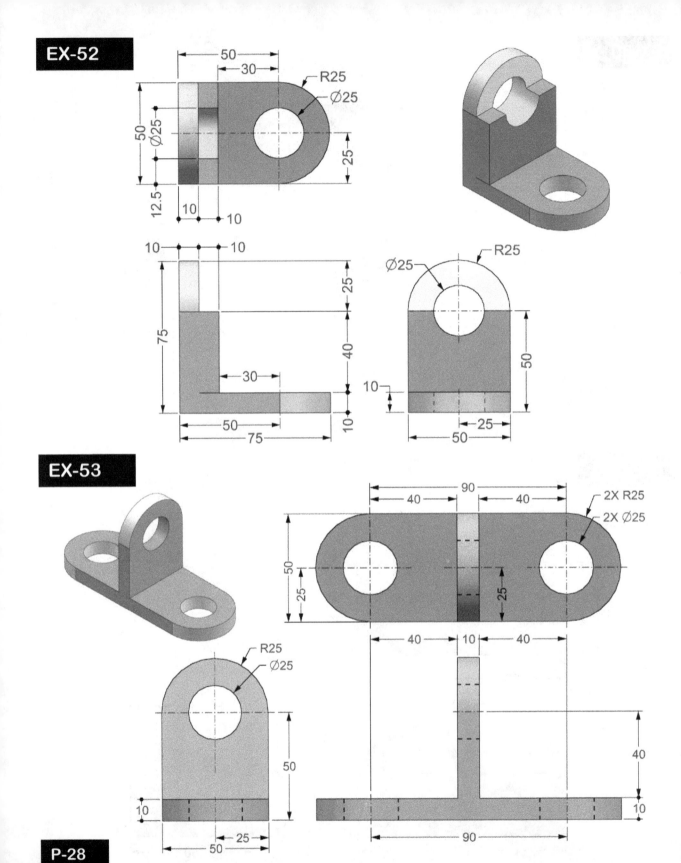

EX-52

50
30
R25
Ø25
50
Ø25
25
12.5
10
10
10
10
25
75
40
30
50
75
10

Ø25
R25
50
10
25
50

EX-53

90
40
40
2X R25
2X Ø25
50
25
25
40
10
40

R25
Ø25
50
10
25
50
40
10
90

P-28

EX-54

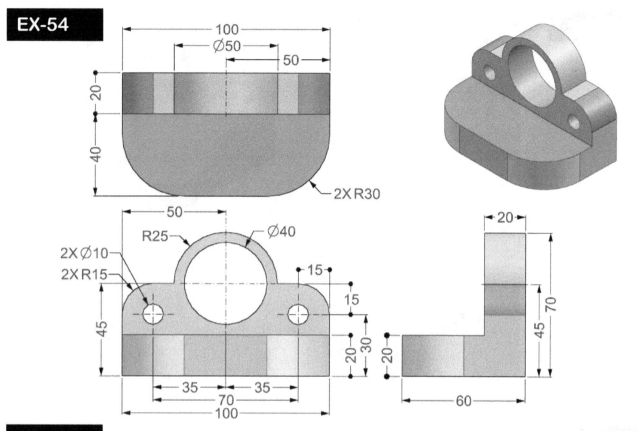

100
Ø50
50
20
40
2X R30

50
R25
Ø40
2X Ø10
2X R15
15
15
45
20
30
35
35
70
100
20
70
45
20
60

EX-55

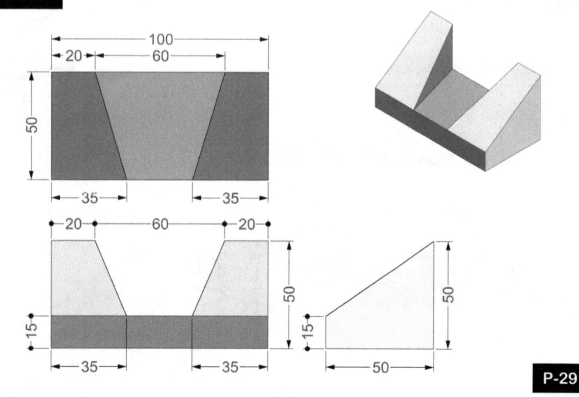

100
20
60
50
35
35

20
60
20
50
15
35
35

50
15
50

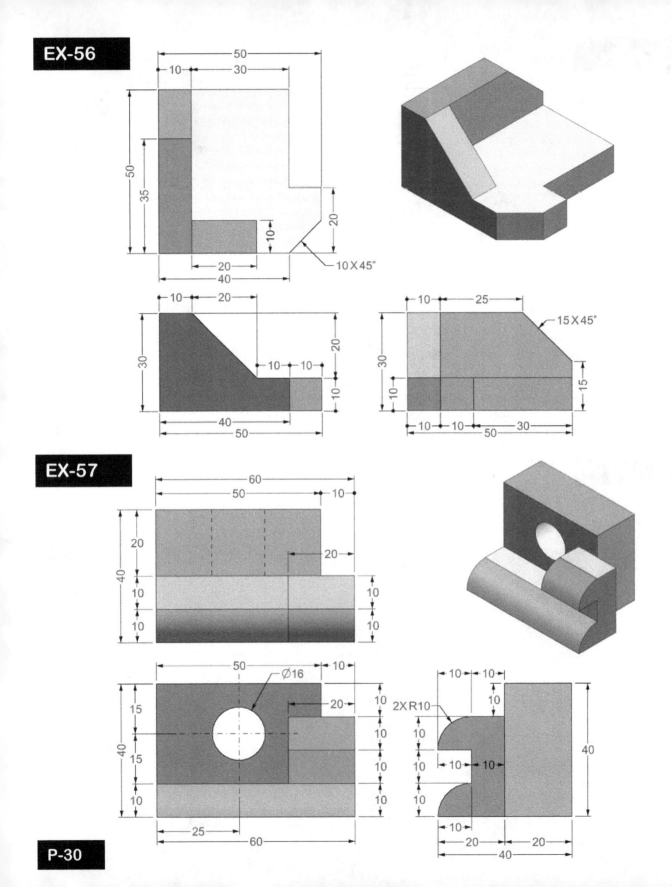

EX-56

50
10 30
50
35
20
10
20
40
10 X 45°

10 20
30
20
10 10
10
40
50

10 25
15 X 45°
30
10
15
10 10 50 30

EX-57

60
50 10
20
20
40
10 10
10 10

50 10
Ø16
15 10
20
40 10
15 10
10
25
60

10 10
2X R10
10
10
10
40
10
10 10
10
20 20
40

P-30

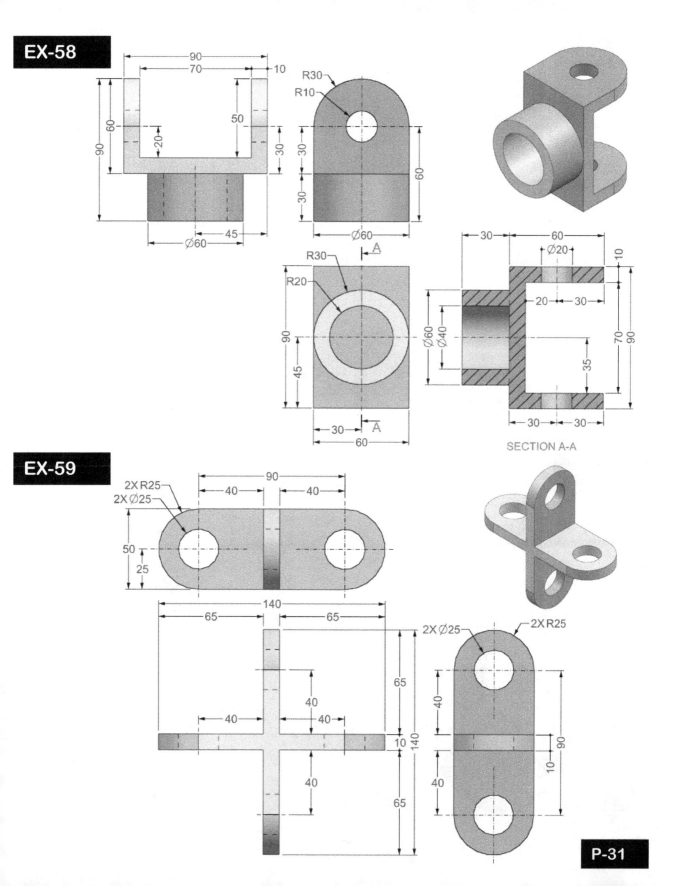

EX-58

EX-59

R30

R10

R30

R20

90

70

10

60

50

20

30

90

30

45

Ø60

30

30

30

Ø60

90

45

30

60

A

A

30

60

Ø20

20

30

Ø60

Ø40

10

70

90

35

30

30

SECTION A-A

2X R25

2X Ø25

90

40

40

50

25

140

65

65

65

40

40

40

40

10

40

65

140

2X Ø25

2X R25

40

90

10

40

P-31

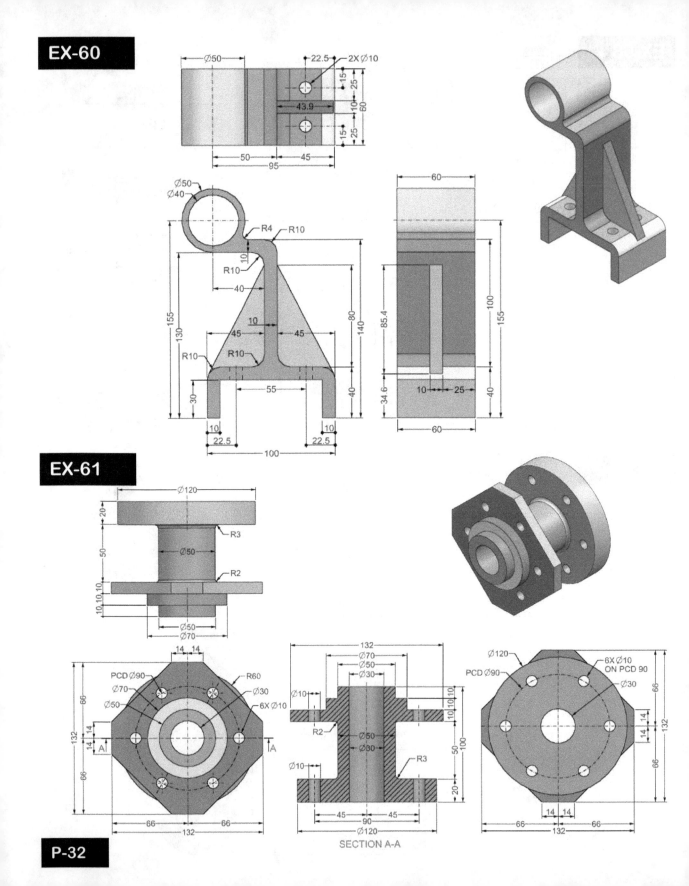

EX-60

EX-61

P-32

SECTION A-A

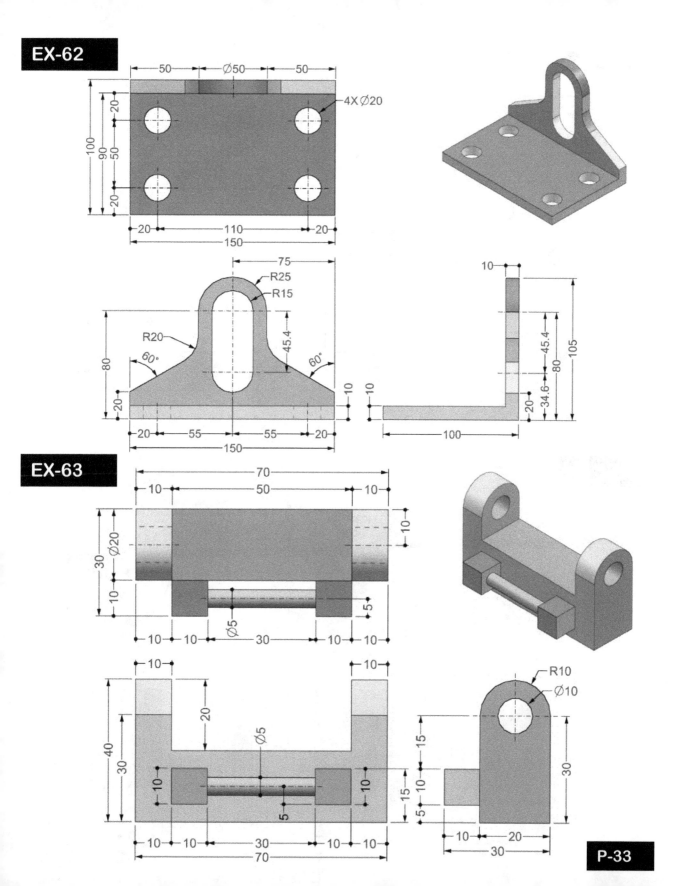

EX-62

50   Ø50   50

4X Ø20

20
100
90
50
20

20   110   20
150

75
R25
R15

R20

60°   60°

80

45.4

10
20

20   55   55   20
150

10

45.4
80
105

10
34.6
20

100

EX-63

70
10   50   10

10

30   Ø20
10

5

10   10   30   10   10
Ø5

10   10

20
40
30

Ø5

10   10

5

10   10   30   10   10
70

R10
Ø10

15
10
5

15

10   20
30

30

P-33

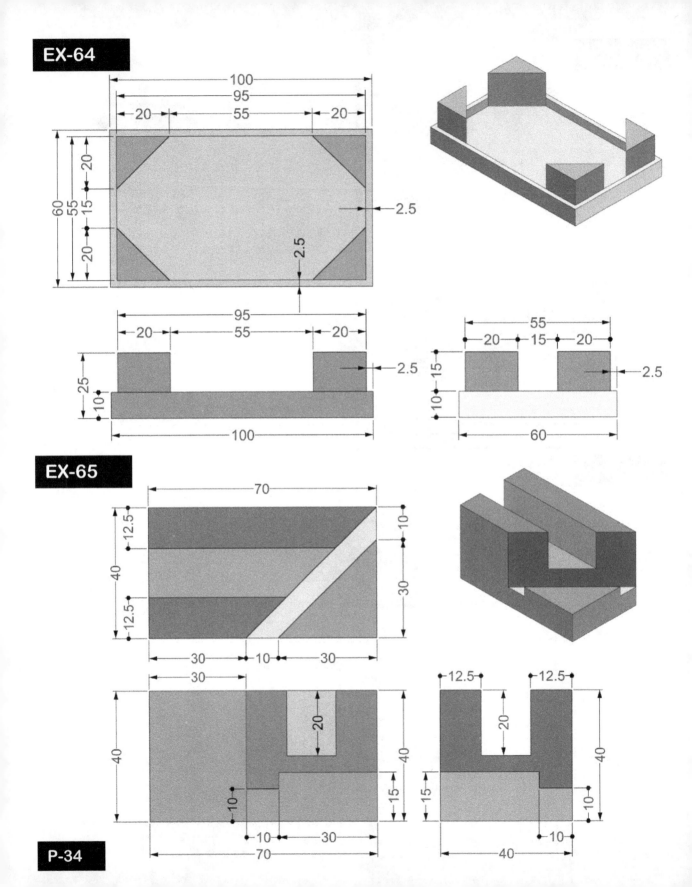

EX-64

EX-65

EX-66

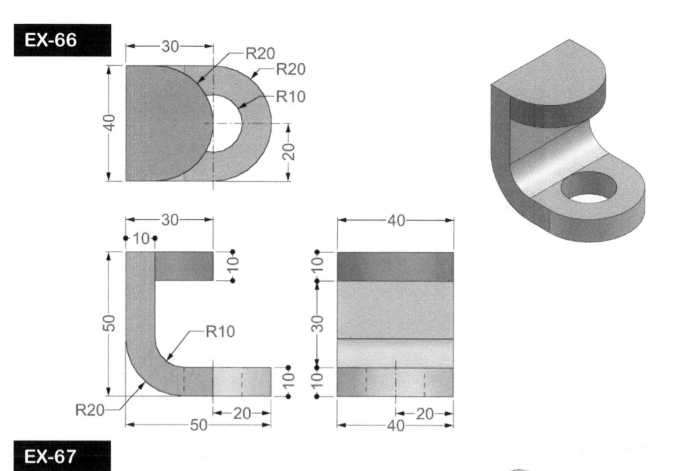

EX-67

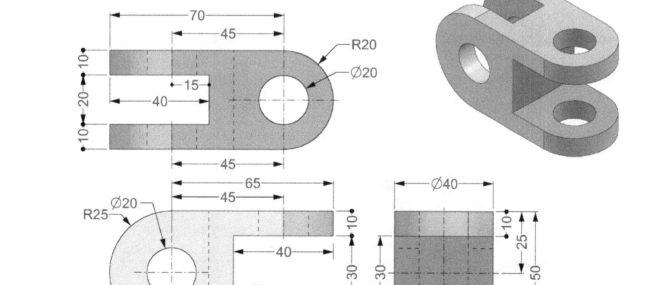

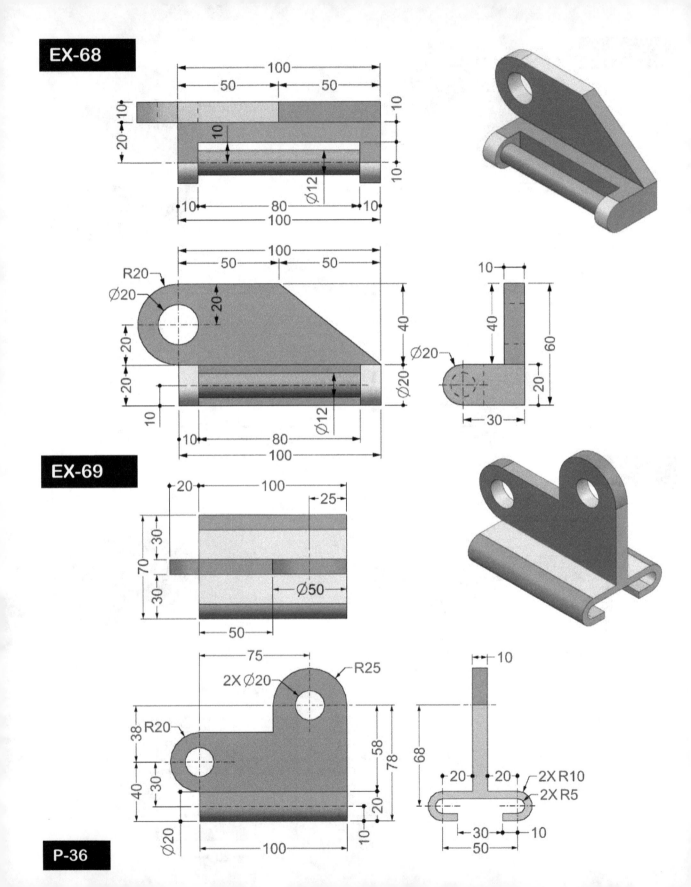

EX-68

EX-69

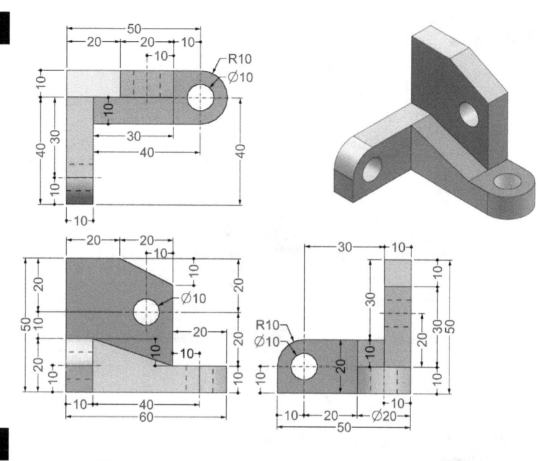

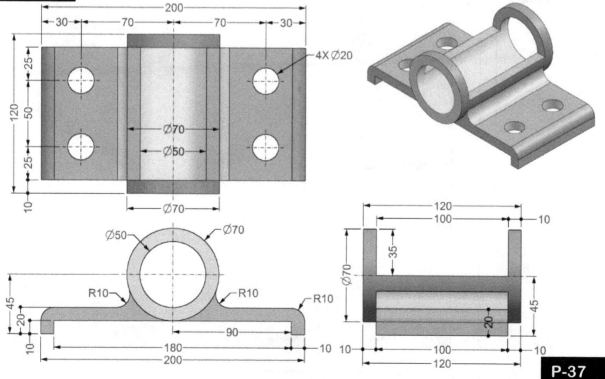

EX-72

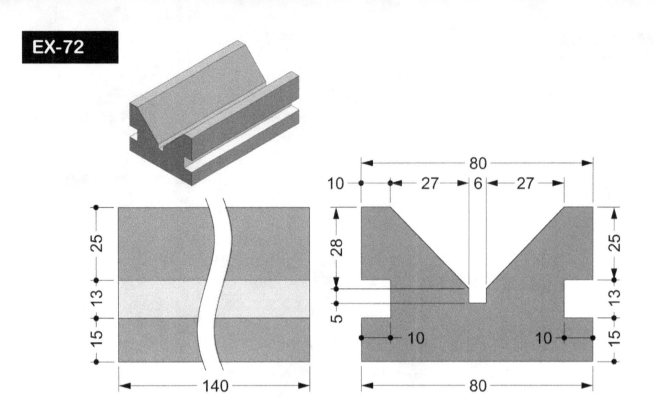

EX-73

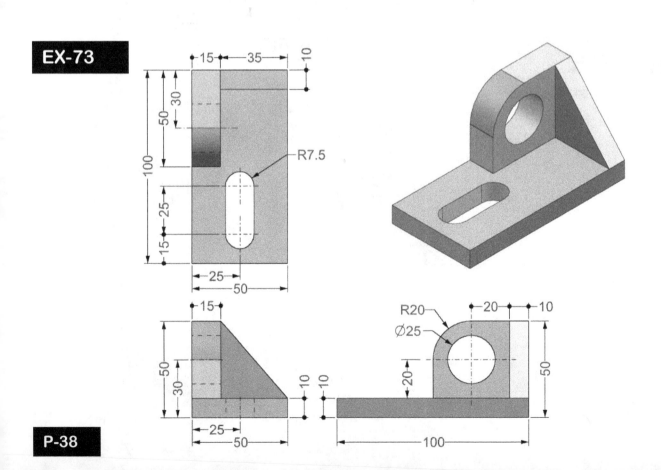

P-38

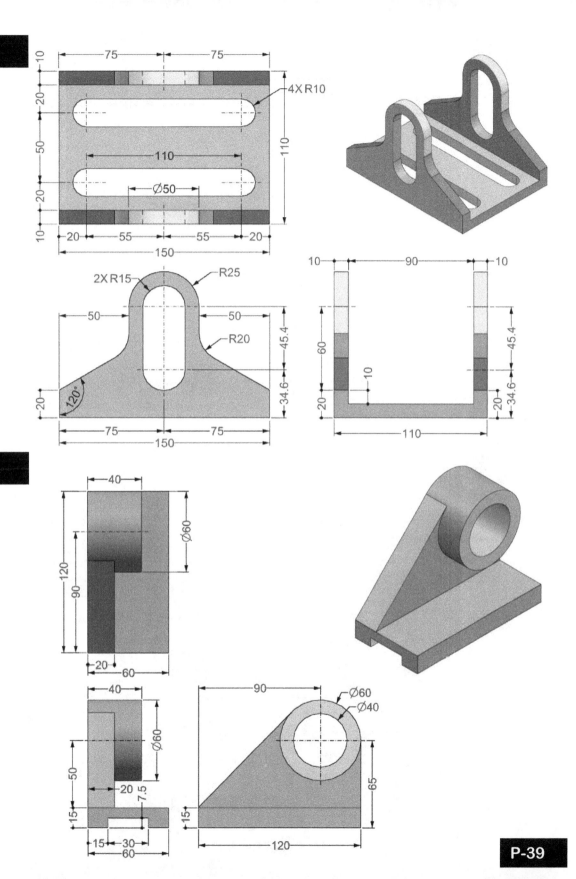

120
70
R20
Ø28
40
10
40
20
10
50

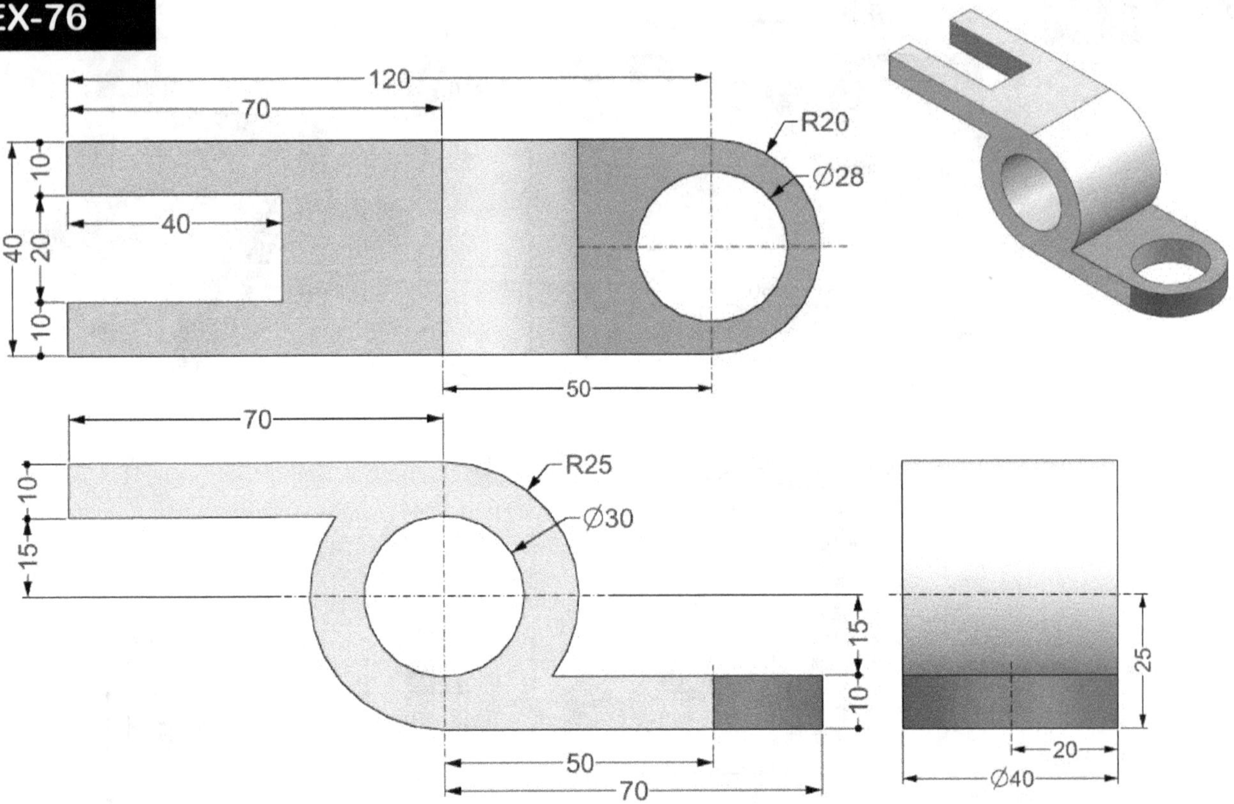

70
R25
10
15
Ø30
15
25
10
50
70
20
Ø40

R15
R25
50
R10
A
A
R5

50
Ø30
R1
30
30
30
20
R4
R2
Ø10
5

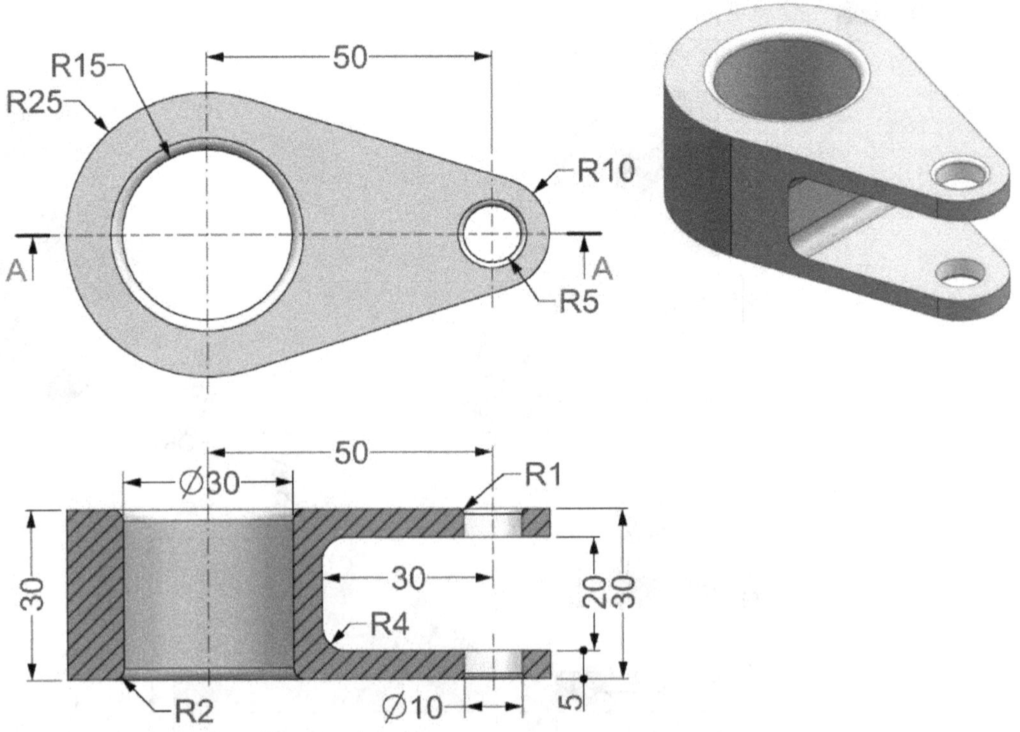

SECTION A-A

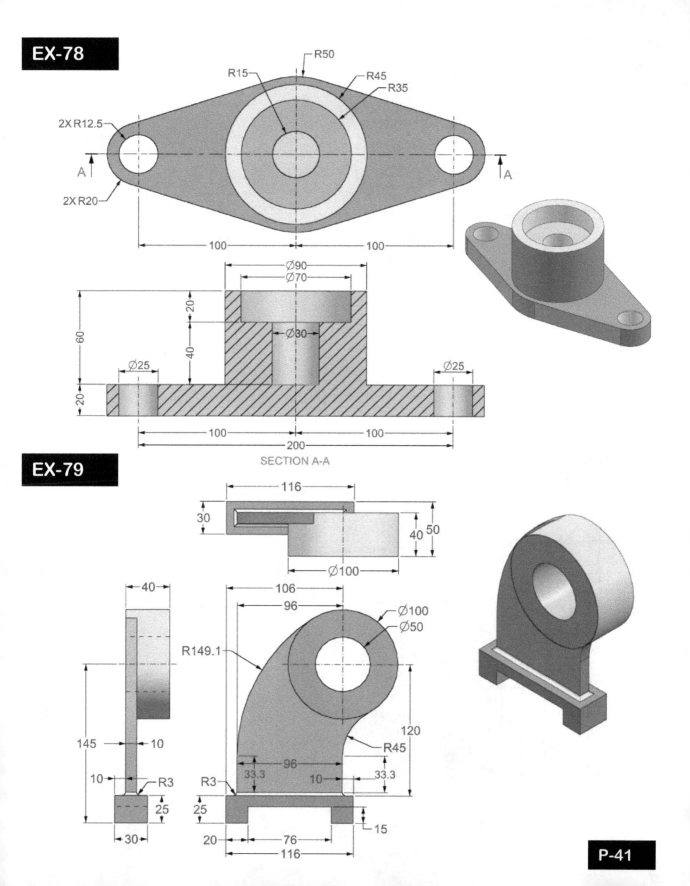

EX-78

R50
R15
R45
R35
2X R12.5
A
A
2X R20
100
100

Ø90
Ø70
20
60
40
Ø30
Ø25
Ø25
20
100
100
200
SECTION A-A

EX-79

116
30
40 50
Ø100

40
106
96
Ø100
Ø50
R149.1
145   10
120
R45
10
R3
10
96
25
R3
33.3   10   33.3
25
30
20
76
15
116

P-41

EX-80

6 HOLES, Ø10
ON DIA 32 PCD

4 HOLES, Ø8.6
ON DIA 54 PCD

Ø70

Ø16

A

A

Ø54

Ø32

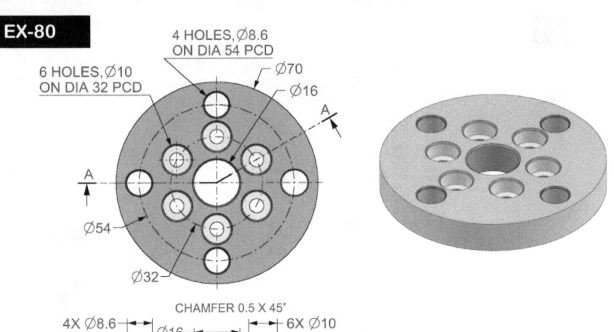

CHAMFER 0.5 X 45°

4X Ø8.6

Ø16

6X Ø10

10

5

5

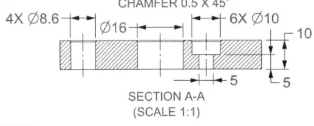

SECTION A-A
(SCALE 1:1)

EX-81

10

207.2

171.6

17.8

6X Ø8.4

87.2

4X R19.4

19.2

254

9.6

106

233.6

254

190.4

109.8

56.4

36.6

38 28

2X R11.6

10

60

10

103.6

147.2

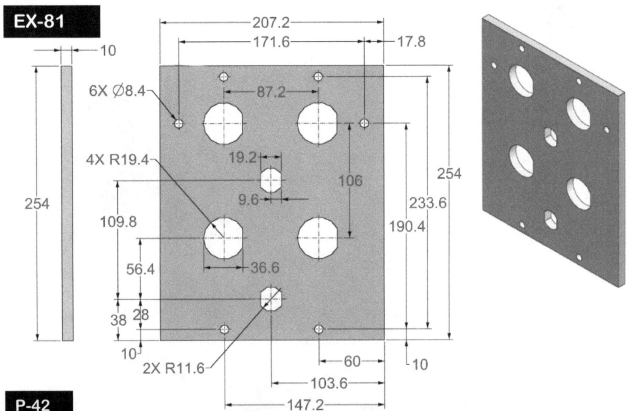

P-42

EX-82

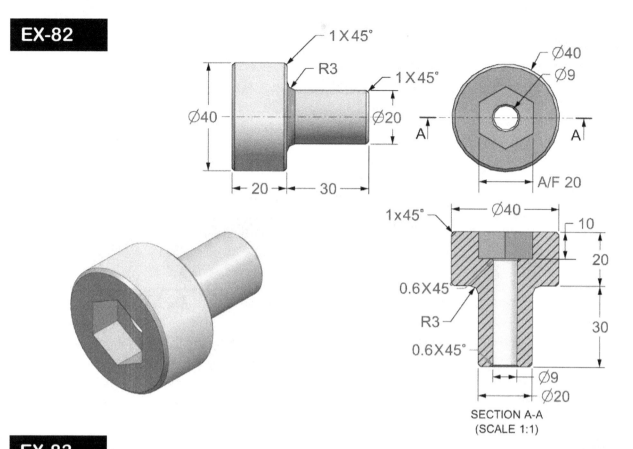

1 X 45°
R3
1 X 45°
Ø40
Ø20
20
30

Ø40
Ø9
A
A
A/F 20

1x45°
Ø40
10
20
0.6X45
R3
30
0.6X45°
Ø9
Ø20

SECTION A-A
(SCALE 1:1)

EX-83

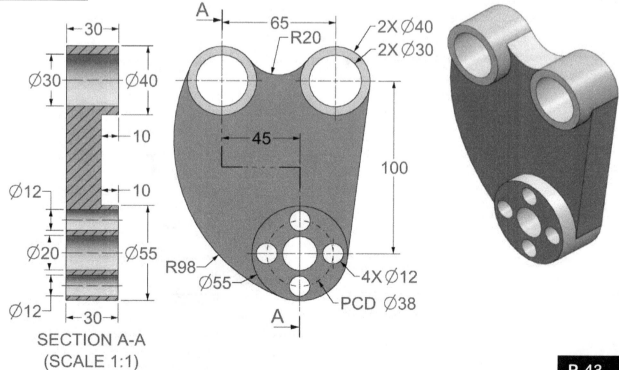

30
Ø30
Ø40
10
10
Ø12
Ø20
Ø55
Ø12
30

SECTION A-A
(SCALE 1:1)

A
65
R20
2X Ø40
2X Ø30
45
100
R98
Ø55
4X Ø12
PCD Ø38
A

EX-84

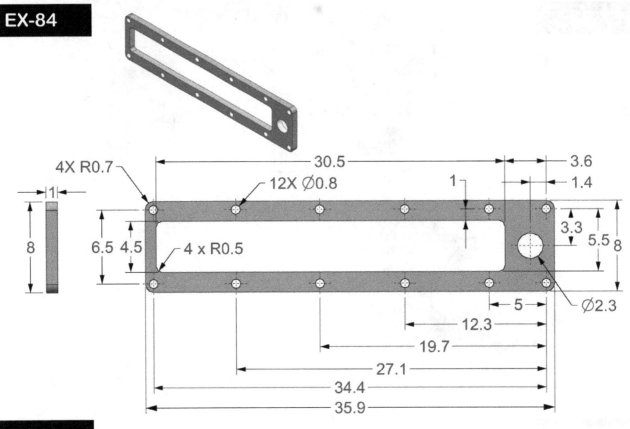

4X R0.7
12X Ø0.8
4 x R0.5
1
30.5
3.6
1.4
6.5 4.5
3.3
5.5 8
8
5
Ø2.3
12.3
19.7
27.1
34.4
35.9
8
1

EX-85

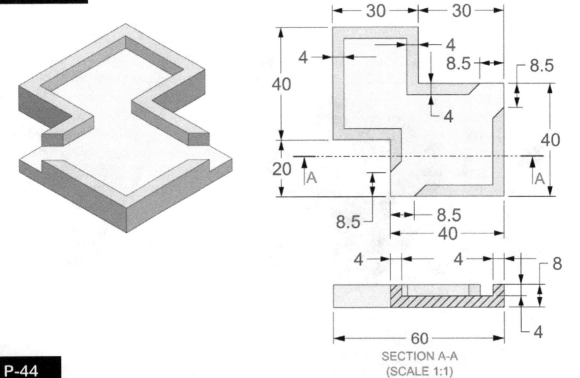

30 30
4
4
8.5 8.5
40
4
40
20
A A
8.5
8.5
40
4 4 8
60
4
SECTION A-A
(SCALE 1:1)

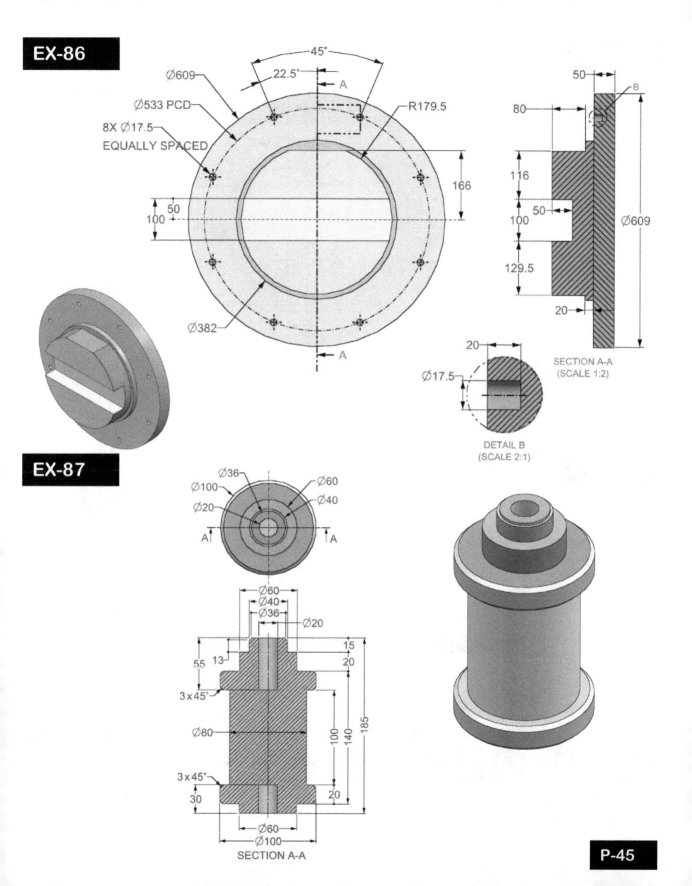

EX-86

Ø609
Ø533 PCD
8X Ø17.5
EQUALLY SPACED
45°
22.5°
A
R179.5
166
50
100
Ø382
A

50
80
B
116
50
100
129.5
20
Ø609

SECTION A-A
(SCALE 1:2)

20
Ø17.5

DETAIL B
(SCALE 2:1)

EX-87

Ø36
Ø100
Ø20
Ø60
Ø40
A
A

Ø60
Ø40
Ø36
Ø20
15
20
55
13
3 x 45°
100
140
185
Ø80
3 x 45°
30
20
Ø60
Ø100
SECTION A-A

P-45

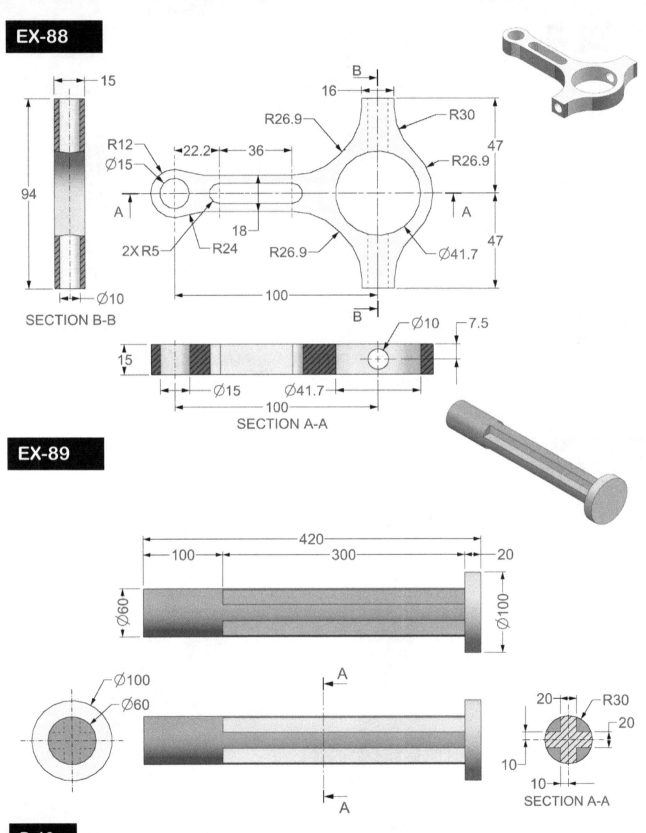

EX-88

R12
Ø15

R26.9

R30

R26.9

15

94

22.2   36

A

A

2X R5   R24

18

R26.9

Ø41.7

16

47

47

100

SECTION B-B

Ø10

Ø10   7.5

15

Ø15   Ø41.7

100

SECTION A-A

EX-89

420

100   300   20

Ø60

Ø100

Ø100

Ø60

A

A

20   R30

20

10

10

SECTION A-A

P-46

EX-90

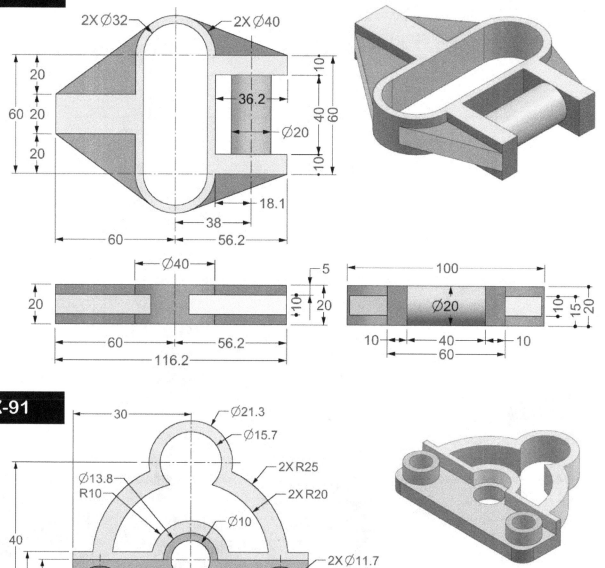

2X ∅32   2X ∅40

20
20
60
20

36.2
∅20

10
40
60
10

18.1
38
60   56.2

∅40
20
60   56.2
116.2

5
10
20

100
∅20
10
15
20

10   40   10
60

EX-91

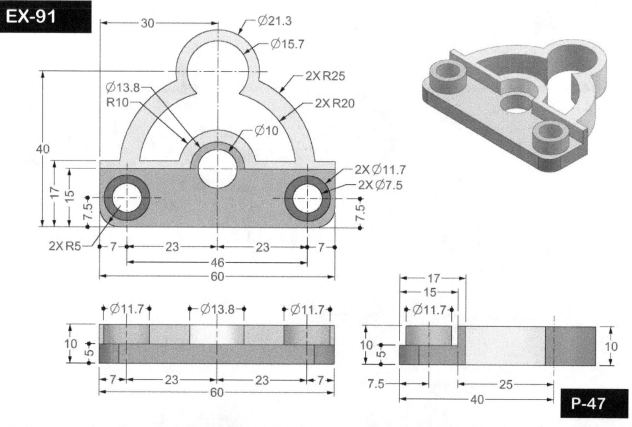

30   ∅21.3
∅15.7
∅13.8
R10
2X R25
2X R20
∅10

40
17
15
7.5
7.5

2X ∅11.7
2X ∅7.5

2X R5   7   23   23   7
46
60

∅11.7   ∅13.8   ∅11.7

10
5

7   23   23   7
60

17
15
∅11.7
10
5
10

7.5   25
40

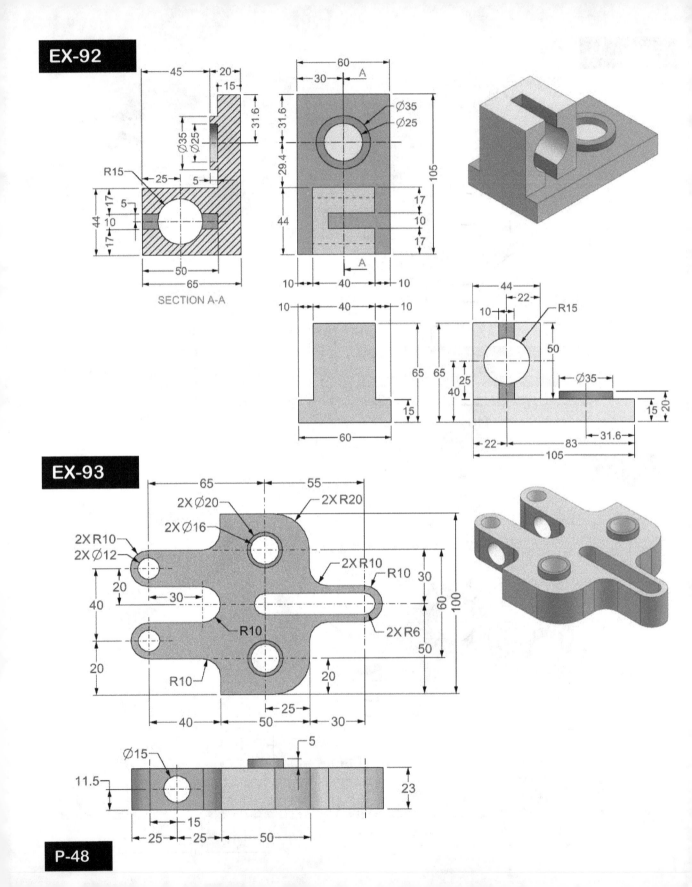

EX-92

45 | 20
15
31.6
Ø35
Ø25
R15
25 | 5
5
17
44
10
17
50
65
SECTION A-A

60
30
A
Ø35
Ø25
31.6
29.4
105
44
17
10
17
A
10 | 40 | 10

10 | 40 | 10
65
15
60

44
22
10
R15
50
65
25
40
Ø35
15 | 20
22 | 83 | 31.6
105

EX-93

65 | 55
2X Ø20
2X R20
2X Ø16
2X R10
2X Ø12
2X R10
R10
30
20
30
40
60
100
30
50
R10
2X R6
20
R10
50
20
40 | 50 | 30
25

Ø15
5
11.5
23
15
25 | 25 | 50

P-48

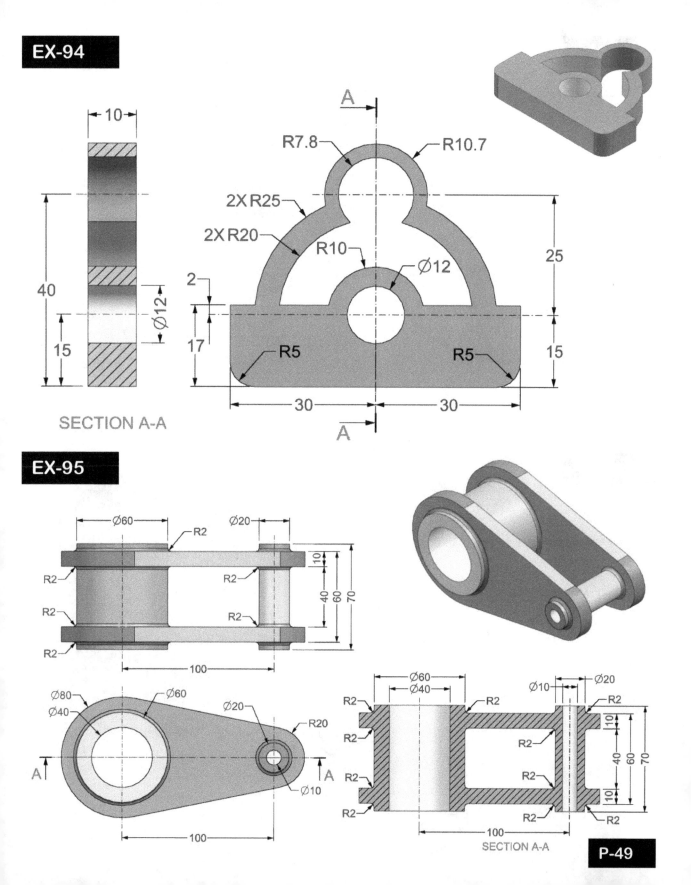

EX-94

10

40

15

Ø12

SECTION A-A

A

R7.8   R10.7

2X R25

2X R20   R10

Ø12

2

17

R5   R5

25

15

30   30

A

EX-95

Ø60   Ø20
R2

R2

R2

R2

R2

10
40
60
70

100

Ø80   Ø60
Ø40

Ø40   Ø20
R20

A   A

Ø10

100

Ø60   Ø20
Ø40   Ø10
R2   R2
R2

R2   R2

R2   R2

R2   R2

10
40
60
70

10

100

SECTION A-A

P-49

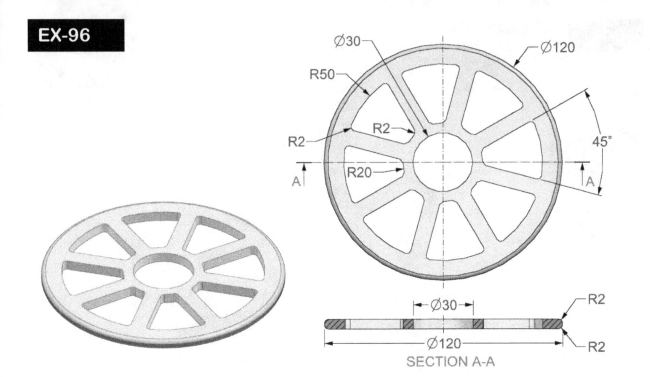

Ø30
Ø120
R50
R2
R2
R2
R20
45°
A
A

Ø30
R2
Ø120
R2
SECTION A-A

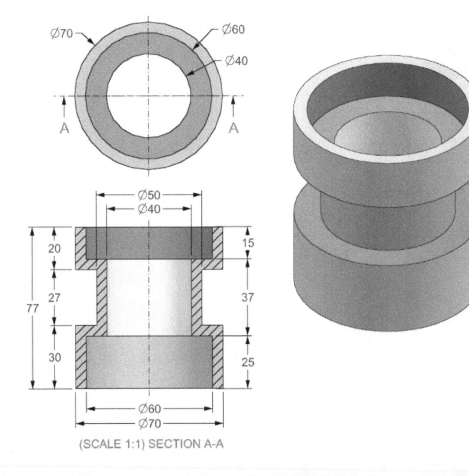

Ø70
Ø60
Ø40
A
A

Ø50
Ø40
20
15
27
37
77
30
25
Ø60
Ø70
(SCALE 1:1) SECTION A-A

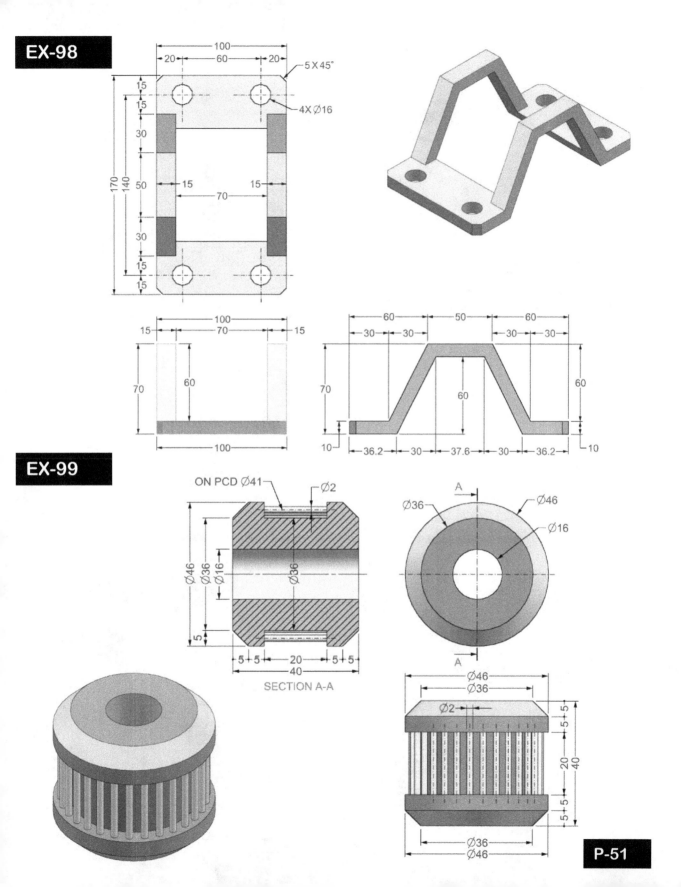

EX-98

100
20 60 20
5 X 45°
4X Ø16
15
15
30
50 15 15
70
30
15
15
170
140

100
15 70 15
70
60
100

60 50 60
30 30 30 30
70
60
60
10
36.2 30 37.6 30 36.2
10

EX-99

ON PCD Ø41
Ø2
A
Ø36
Ø46
Ø16

Ø46
Ø36
Ø16
Ø36

5
5 5 20 5 5
40
SECTION A-A

A

Ø46
Ø36
Ø2
5 5
5
20
40
5 5
Ø36
Ø46

P-51

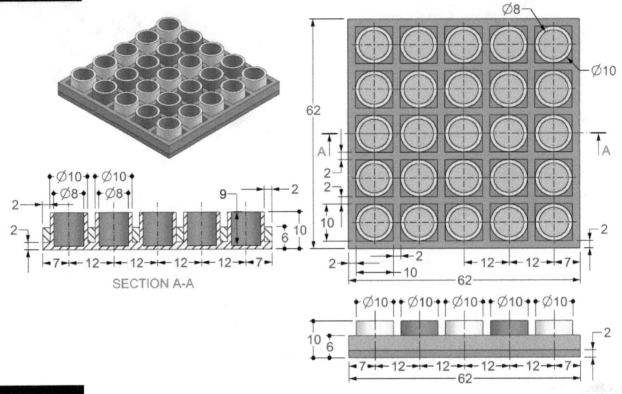

SECTION A-A

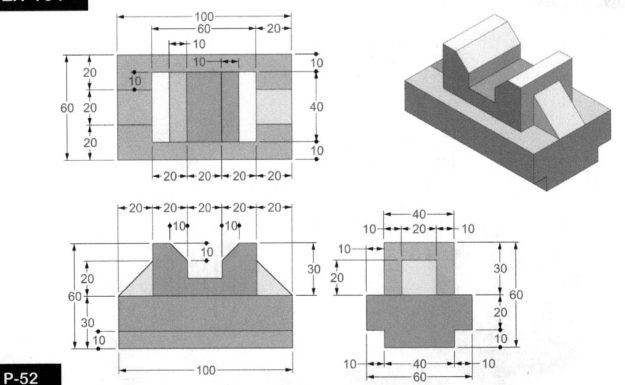

EX-102

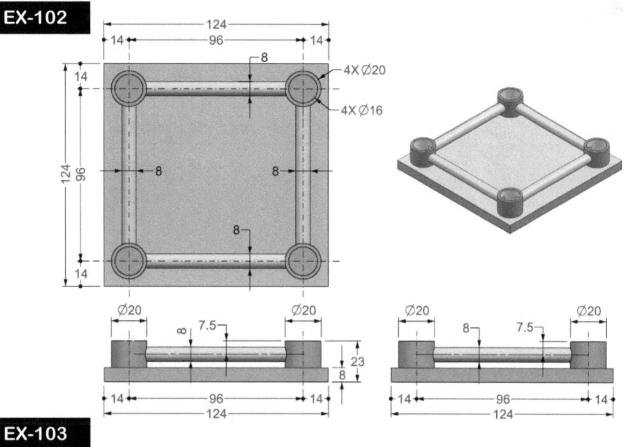

EX-103

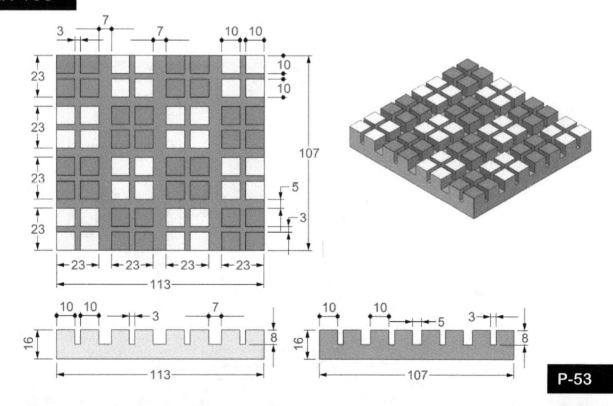

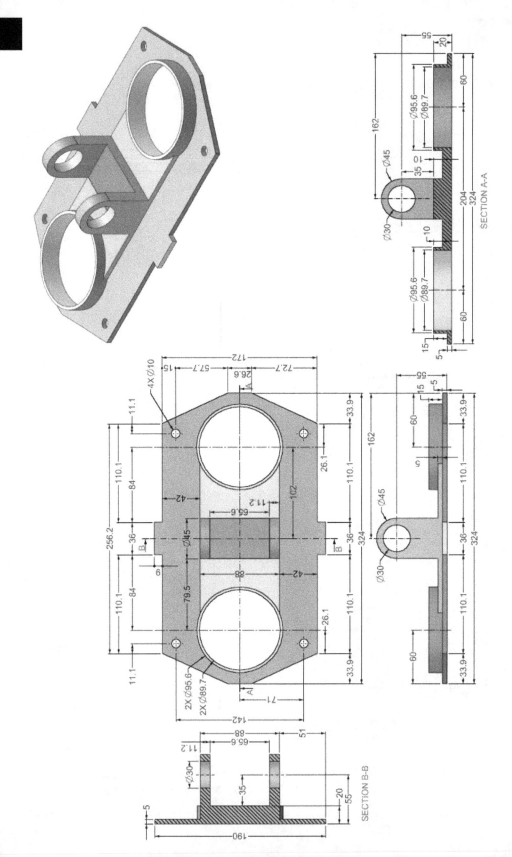

SECTION A-A

SECTION B-B

EX-105

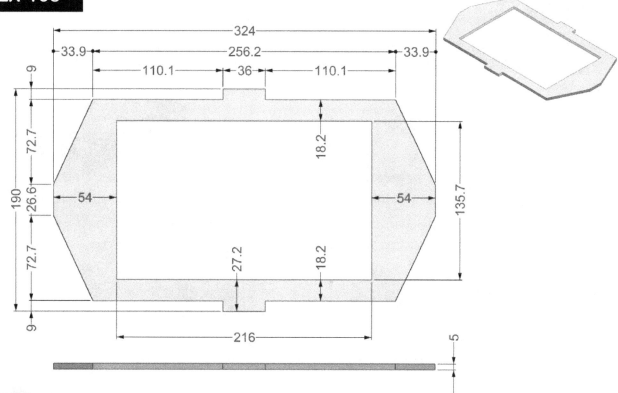

EX-106

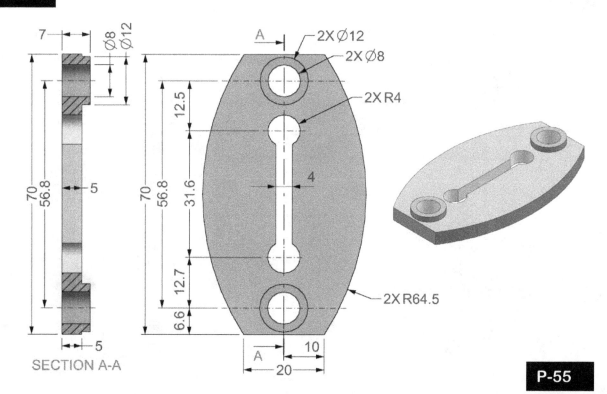

2X Ø12
2X Ø8
2X R4
4
2X R64.5

SECTION A-A

EX-107

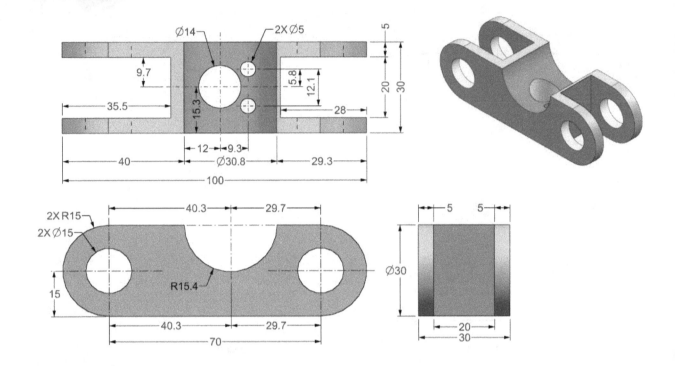

EX-108

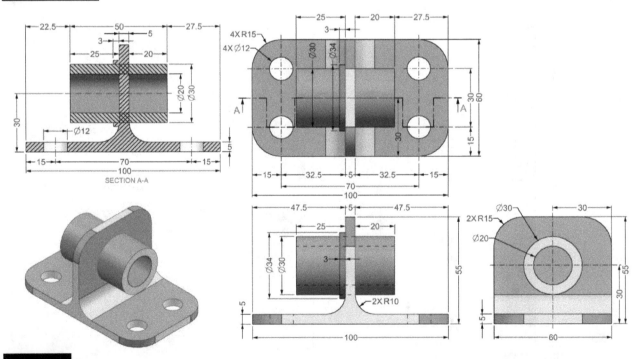

SECTION A-A

P-56

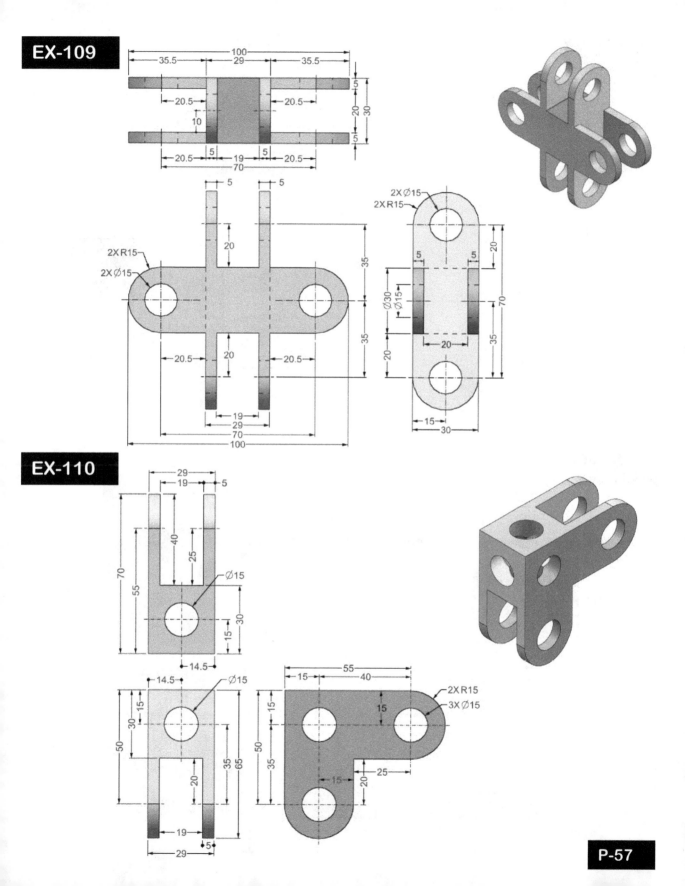

EX-109

EX-110

P-57

EX-111

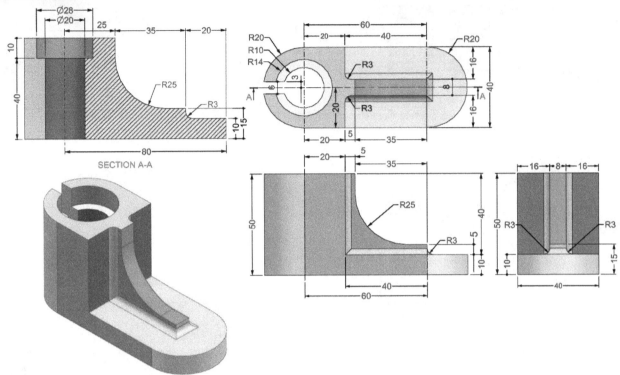

SECTION A-A

EX-112

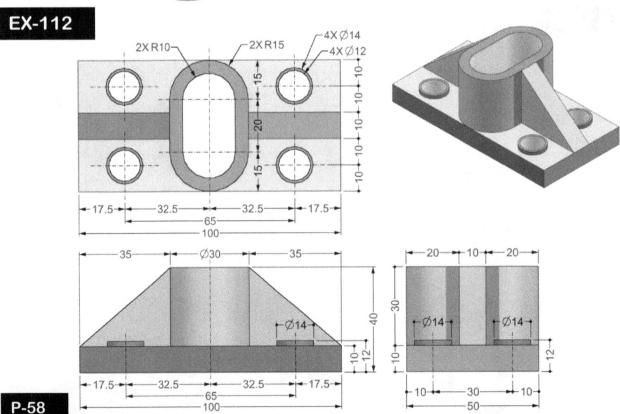

EX-113

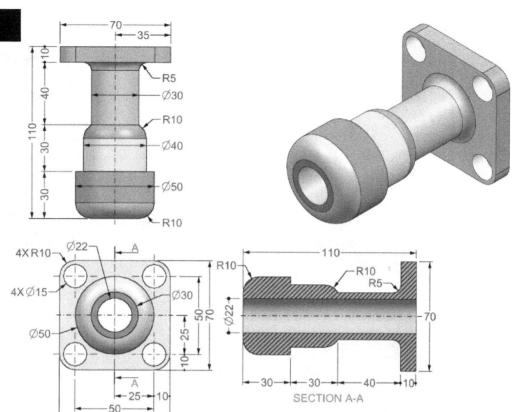

4X R10 Ø22 A
4X Ø15
Ø50 Ø30
Ø50
70
50
25
10
A
25 10
50
70

70
35
10
R5
Ø30
40
110
R10
30
Ø40
30
Ø50
R10

110
R10
R10
R5
Ø22
70
30 30 40 10
SECTION A-A

EX-114

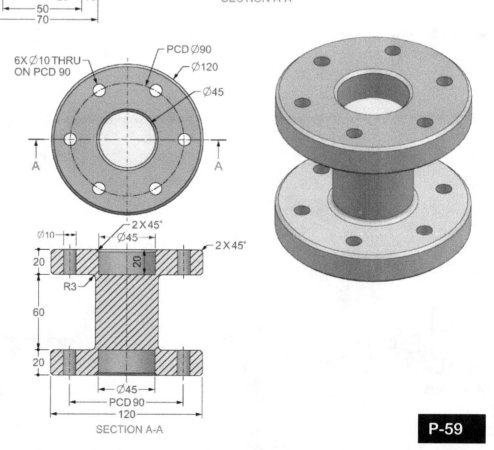

6X Ø10 THRU
ON PCD 90
PCD Ø90
Ø120
Ø45

A A

2 X 45°
Ø45
20
Ø10
20
R3
2 X 45°
60
20
Ø45
PCD 90
120
SECTION A-A

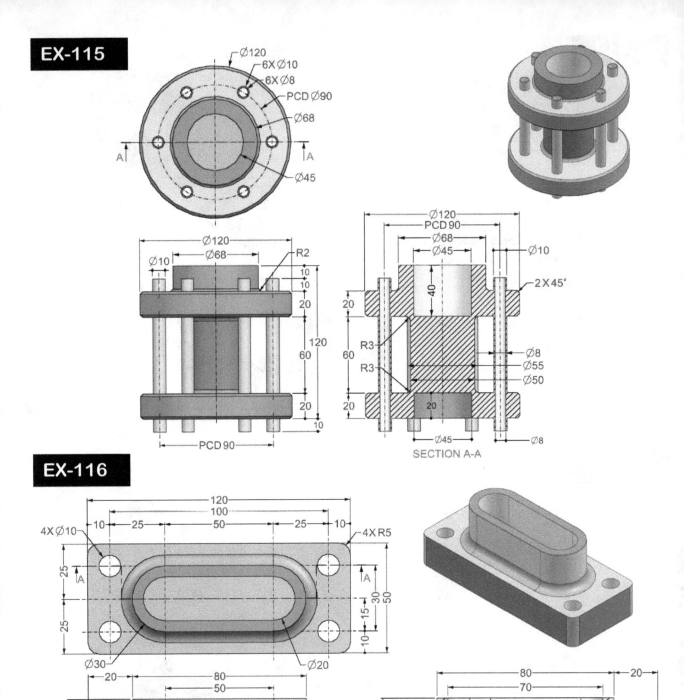

EX-115

Ø120
6X Ø10
6X Ø8
PCD Ø90
Ø68
Ø45
A
A

Ø120
Ø68
Ø10
R2
10
10
20
120
60
20
10
PCD 90

Ø120
PCD 90
Ø68
Ø45
Ø10
40
20
R3
60
R3
20
20
Ø45
2X45°
Ø8
Ø55
Ø50
Ø8

SECTION A-A

EX-116

120
100
10 25 50 25 10
4X Ø10
4X R5
25
A
A
25
30
50
10 15
Ø30
Ø20

20
80
50
45
20
R5
120

80
20
70
25
Ø10
30
R5
20
10
100
120

SECTION A-A

P-60

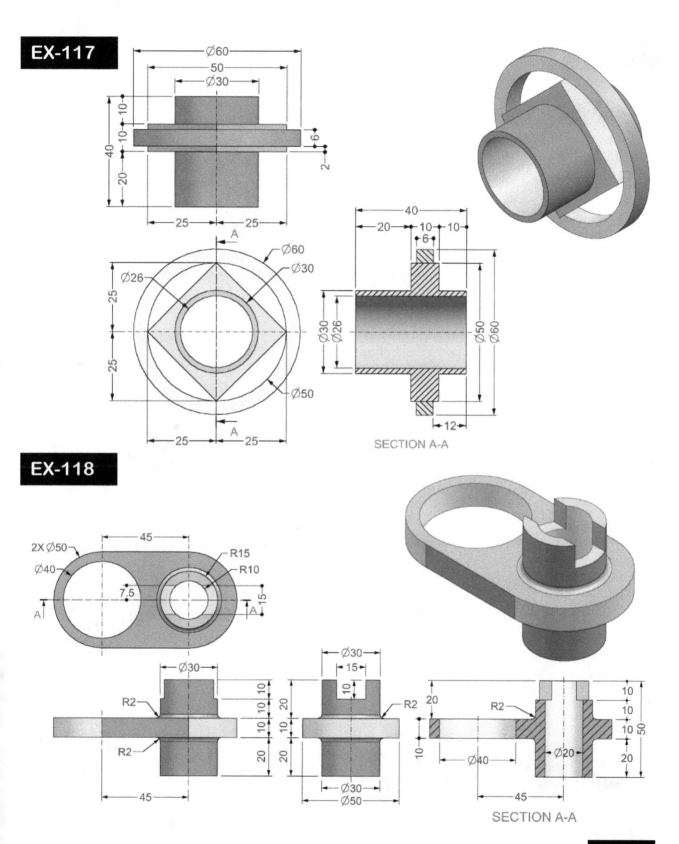

EX-117

Ø60
50
Ø30
40
10
10
20
6
2
25
25

A

Ø26
Ø60
Ø30
25
25
Ø50

25
25

A

40
20
10
10
6
Ø30
Ø26
Ø50
Ø60
12

SECTION A-A

EX-118

45
2X Ø50
R15
Ø40
R10
7.5
15
A
A

Ø30
R2
10
10
10
10
10
20
R2
20
45

Ø30
15
10
20
10
10
R2
20
Ø30
Ø50

20
R2
10
10
10
50
10
Ø40
Ø20
20
45

SECTION A-A

P-61

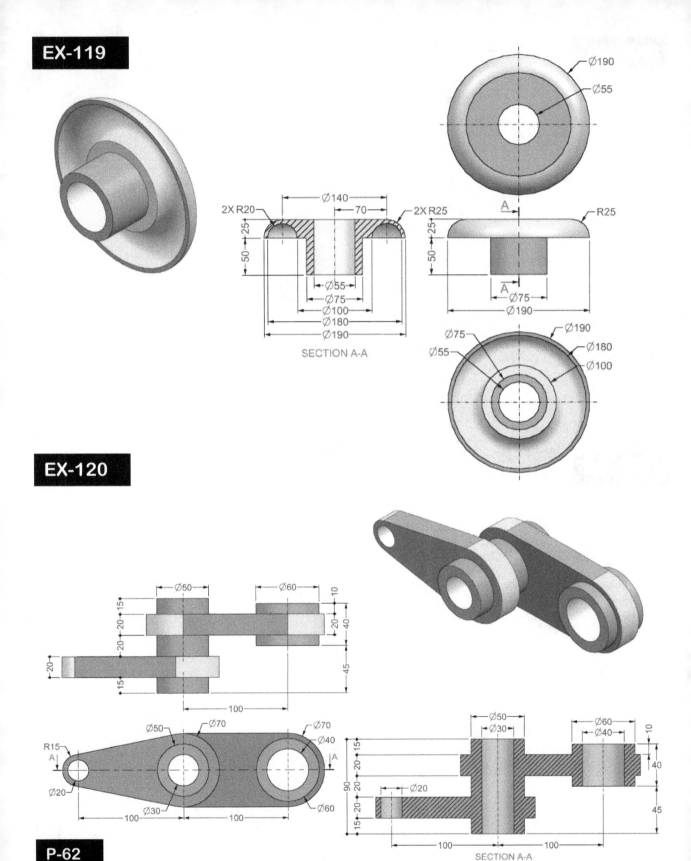

EX-119

Ø190
Ø55

Ø140
70
2X R20
2X R25
2X R25
A
R25
50
25
50
25
Ø55
Ø75
Ø100
Ø180
Ø190
SECTION A-A
A
Ø75
Ø190
Ø190
Ø75
Ø180
Ø55
Ø100

EX-120

Ø50
Ø60
10
15
20
20
20
40
20
20
45
15
100

Ø50
Ø70
Ø70
R15
A
Ø40
Ø50
Ø30
Ø60
A
Ø20
Ø30
Ø60
100
100

Ø50
Ø30
Ø60
Ø40
10
15
20
20
20
40
90
20
Ø20
45
15
100
100
SECTION A-A

P-62

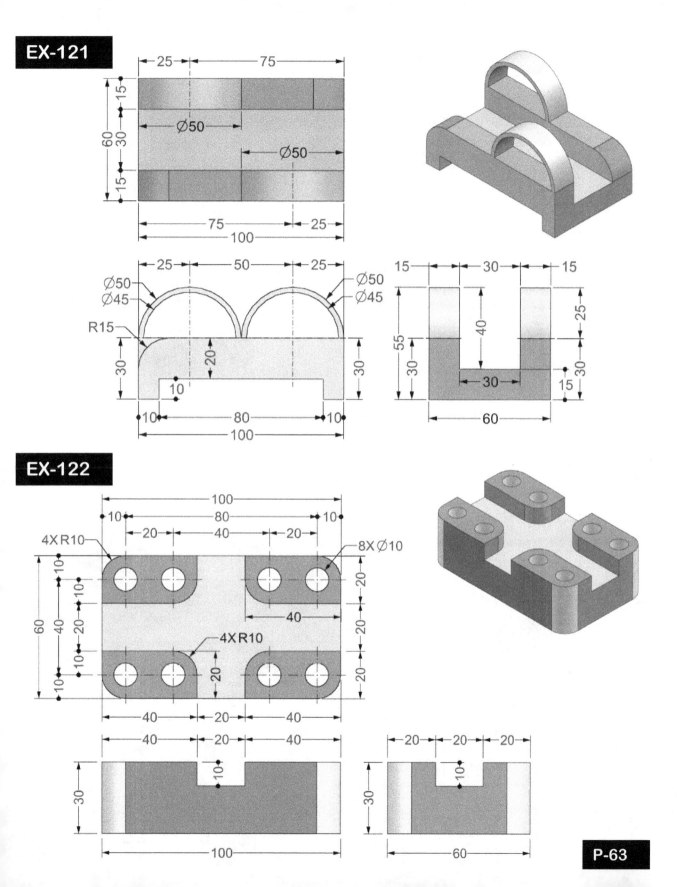

EX-121

EX-122

EX-123

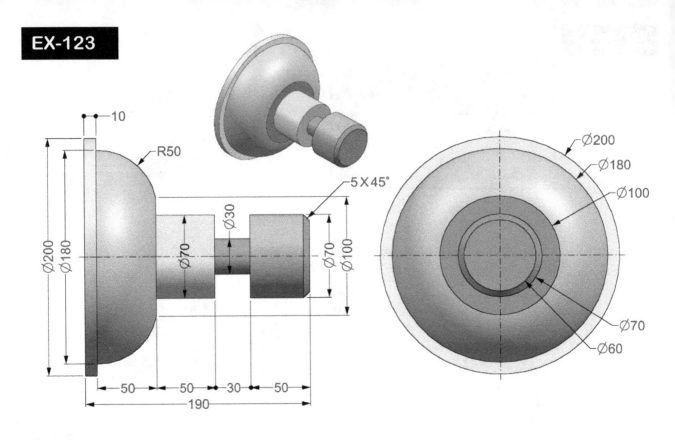

10
R50
5 X 45°
Ø30
Ø70
Ø70
Ø100
Ø200
Ø180
50 50 30 50
190

Ø200
Ø180
Ø100
Ø70
Ø60

EX-124

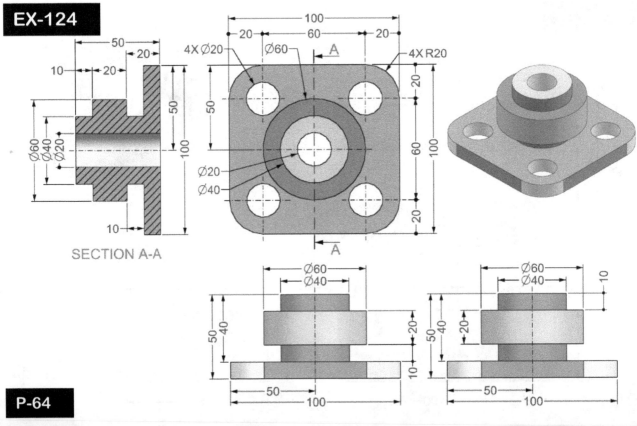

50
20
10 20
4X Ø20
Ø60
A
4X R20
Ø60
Ø40
Ø20
50
100
Ø20
Ø40
10
100
20
60
20
20
60
20
100
A
SECTION A-A

Ø60
Ø40
50
40
20
50
10
100

Ø60
Ø40
10
50
40
20
50
100

EX-125

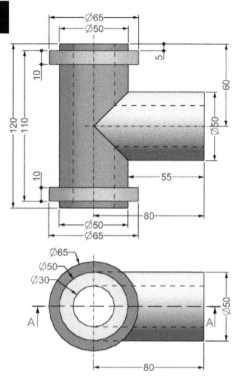

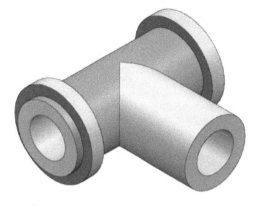

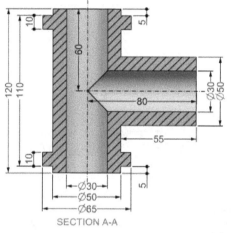

SECTION A-A

EX-126

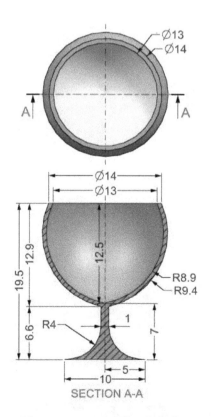

Ø13
Ø14

Ø14
Ø13
12.5
19.5
12.9
R8.9
R9.4
6.6
R4
1
7
5
10

SECTION A-A

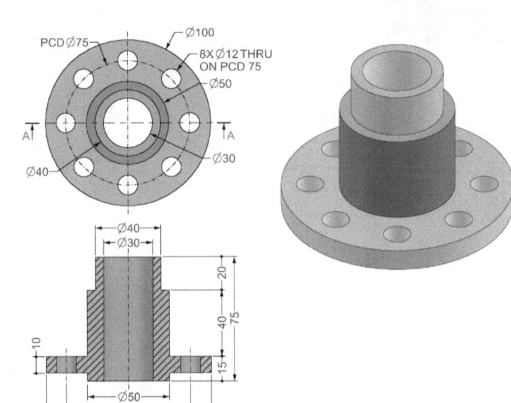

Ø100
PCD Ø75
8X Ø12 THRU
ON PCD 75
Ø50
Ø30
Ø40

Ø40
Ø30
20
40
75
10
15
Ø50
75
Ø100

SECTION A-A

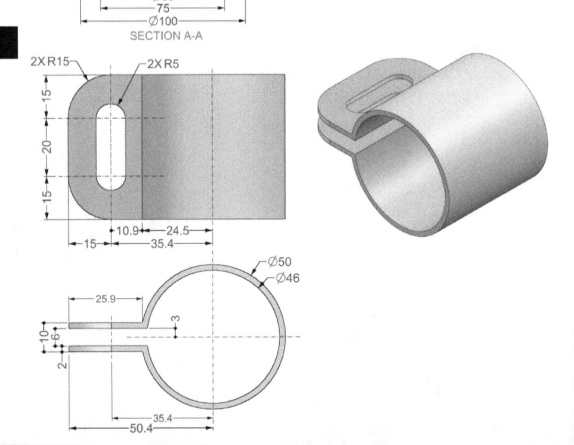

2X R15
2X R5
15
20
15
10.9
24.5
15
35.4

Ø50
Ø46
25.9
3
10
6
2
35.4
50.4

EX-129

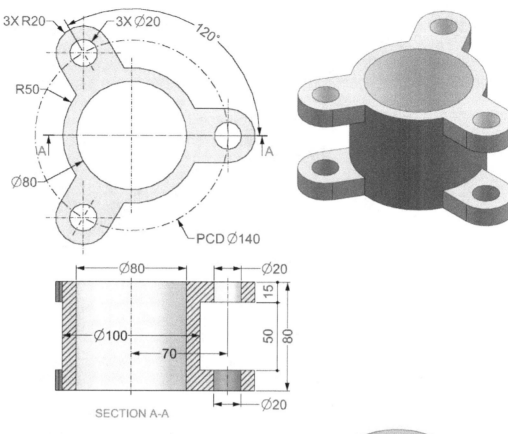

3X R20   3X Ø20   120°

R50

Ø80

PCD Ø140

Ø80   Ø20

15

50   80

Ø100

70

Ø20

SECTION A-A

EX-130

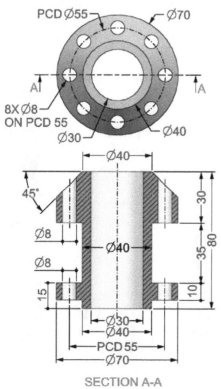

PCD Ø55   Ø70

8X Ø8
ON PCD 55

Ø30   Ø40

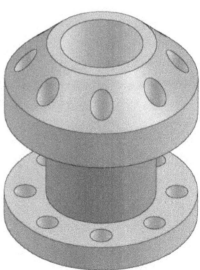

Ø40

45°

30

Ø8

Ø40   80

Ø8   35

15   10

Ø30

Ø40

PCD 55

Ø70

SECTION A-A

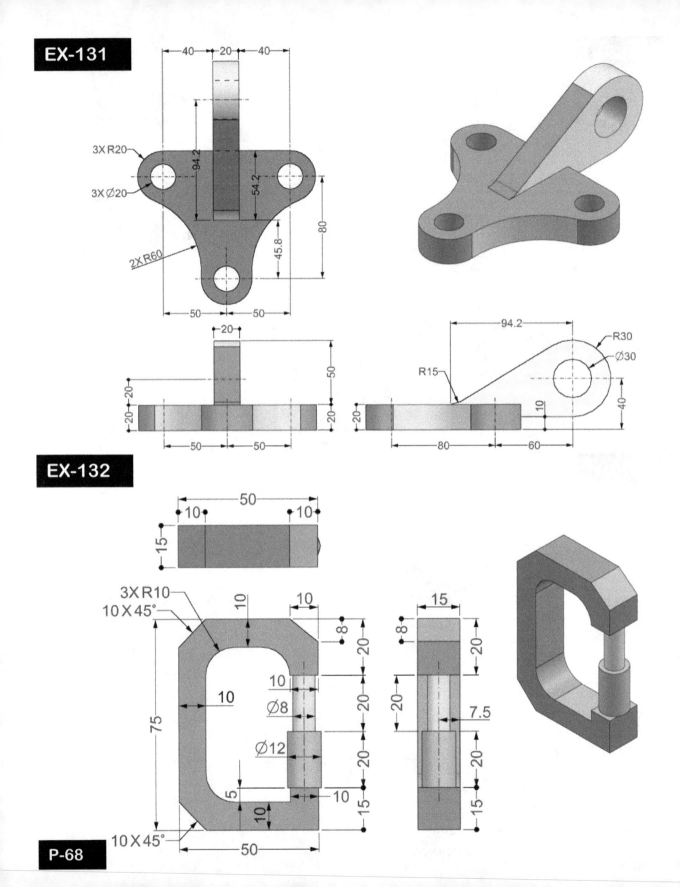

EX-131

3X R20
3X Ø20
2X R60
94.2
54.2
80
45.8
40
20
40
20
50
50
20
50
50
20
20
50
20

94.2
R30
Ø30
R15
20
10
40
80
60

EX-132

50
10
10
15

3X R10
10 X 45°
10
75
10
Ø8
Ø12
5
10
10 X 45°
50

10
8
20
20
20
15

15
8
20
20
20
15

20
7.5

P-68

EX-133

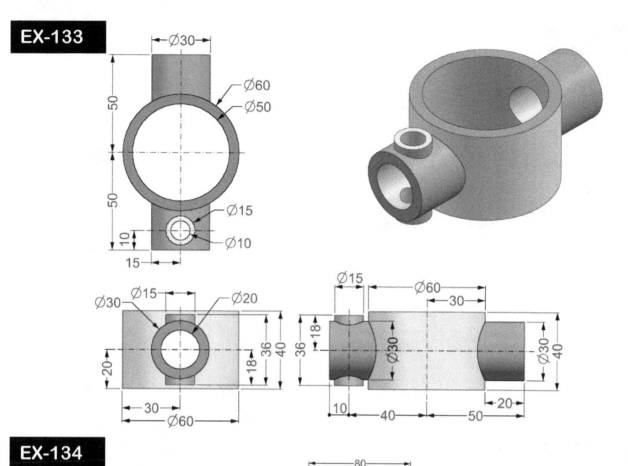

EX-134

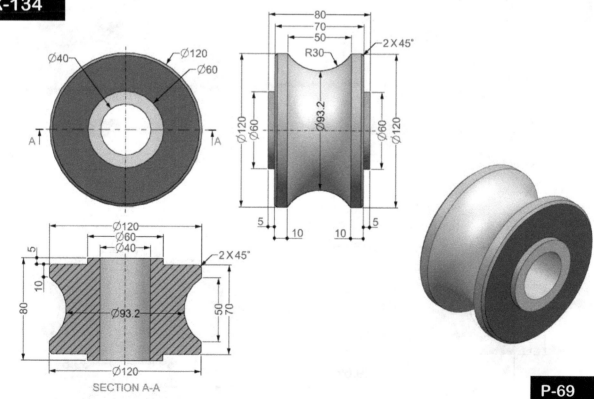

SECTION A-A

P-69

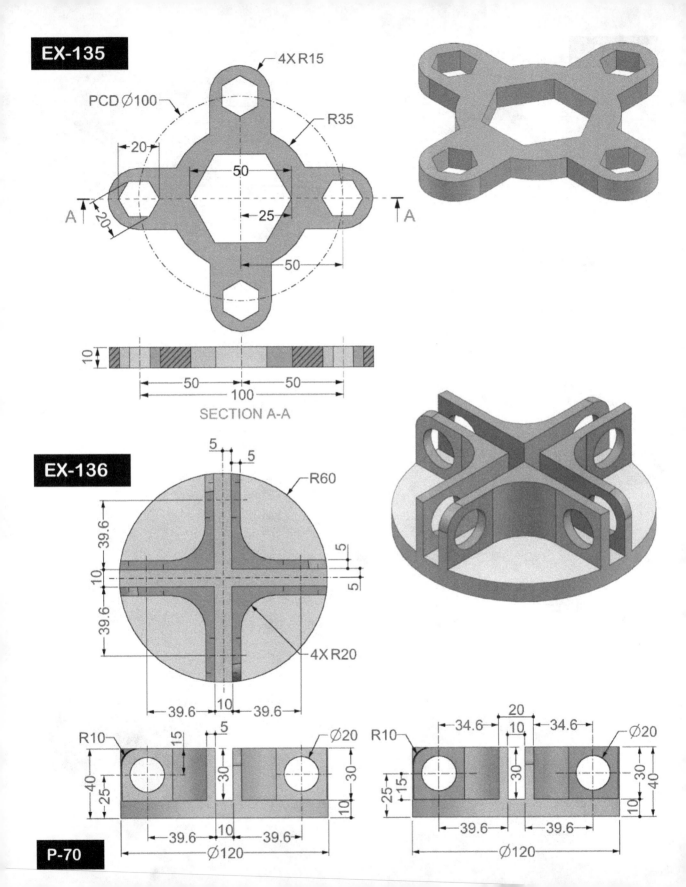

EX-135

4X R15

PCD Ø100

R35

20

50

25

50

A

20

A

10

50

50

100

SECTION A-A

EX-136

5

5

R60

39.6

39.6

10

5

5

39.6

10

4X R20

39.6

R10

15

5

Ø20

40

30

25

30

10

39.6

10

39.6

Ø120

R10

20

34.6

10

34.6

Ø20

30

25

15

30

40

10

39.6

39.6

Ø120

P-70

EX-137

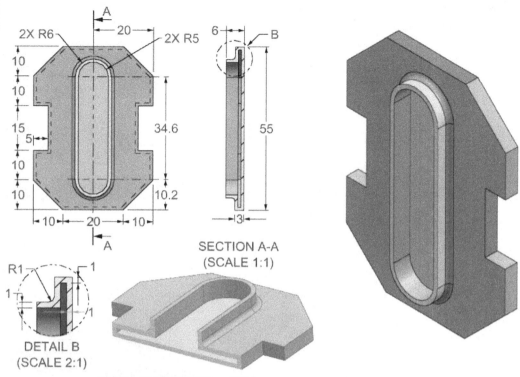

2X R6
2X R5
20
6
B
10
10
34.6
55
15
5
10.2
10
10
10 20 10
3
A
A

SECTION A-A
(SCALE 1:1)

R1
1
1
1

DETAIL B
(SCALE 2:1)

SHELL THICKNESS = 1MM
ALL INSIDE WALL THICKNESS

EX-138

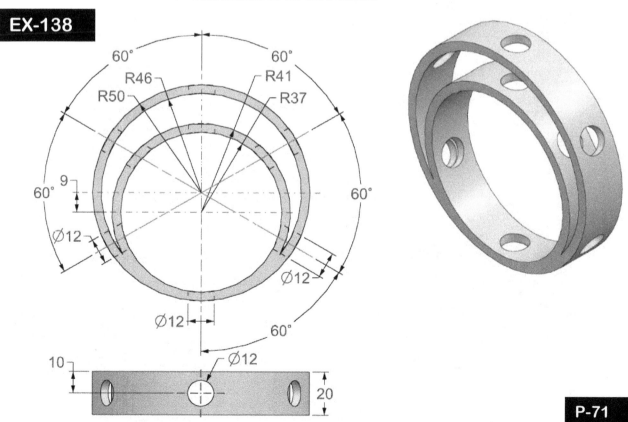

60°   60°
R46   R41
R50   R37

60° 9   60°
Ø12
Ø12
Ø12
60°

10   Ø12
20

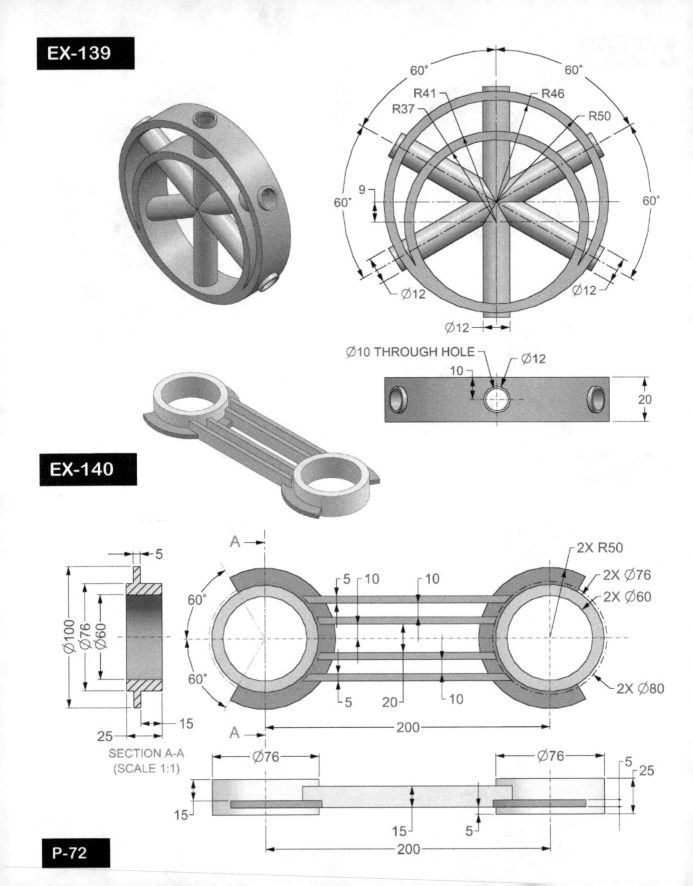

EX-139

60° 60°
R41 R46
R37 R50
60° 9 60°
60° 60°
Ø12 Ø12
Ø12

Ø10 THROUGH HOLE Ø12
10
20

EX-140

SECTION A-A
(SCALE 1:1)

A
60°
5 10 10
60°
5 20 10
A
200

Ø100
Ø76
Ø60
5
15
25

2X R50
2X Ø76
2X Ø60
2X Ø80

Ø76 Ø76
5 25
15
15 5
200

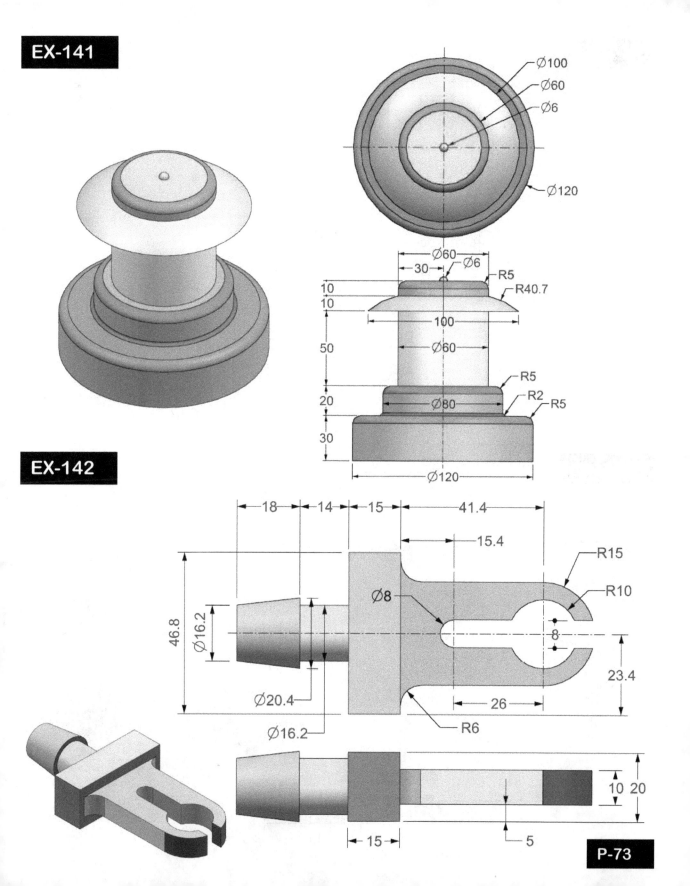

EX-141

⌀100
⌀60
⌀6
⌀120

⌀60
30
⌀6
R5
10
10
R40.7
100
⌀60
50
R5
20
⌀80
R2 R5
30
⌀120

EX-142

18
14
15
41.4
15.4
R15
R10
⌀8
46.8
⌀16.2
8
⌀20.4
23.4
⌀16.2
26
R6
10 20
15
5

P-73

EX-143

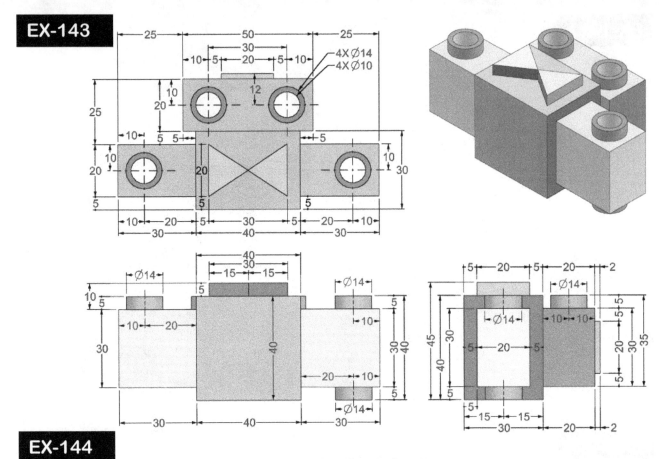

EX-144

8X Ø26 THRU HOLE
ON PCD 160

PCD Ø160

Ø80   Ø60

PCD Ø160

19.3

19.3

30

20.6°

60

20.6°

80

SECTION A-A

25   19.3   9.7

10   5   10   20

8X Ø12

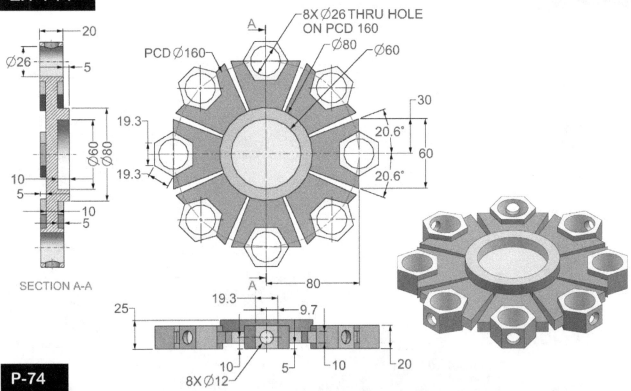

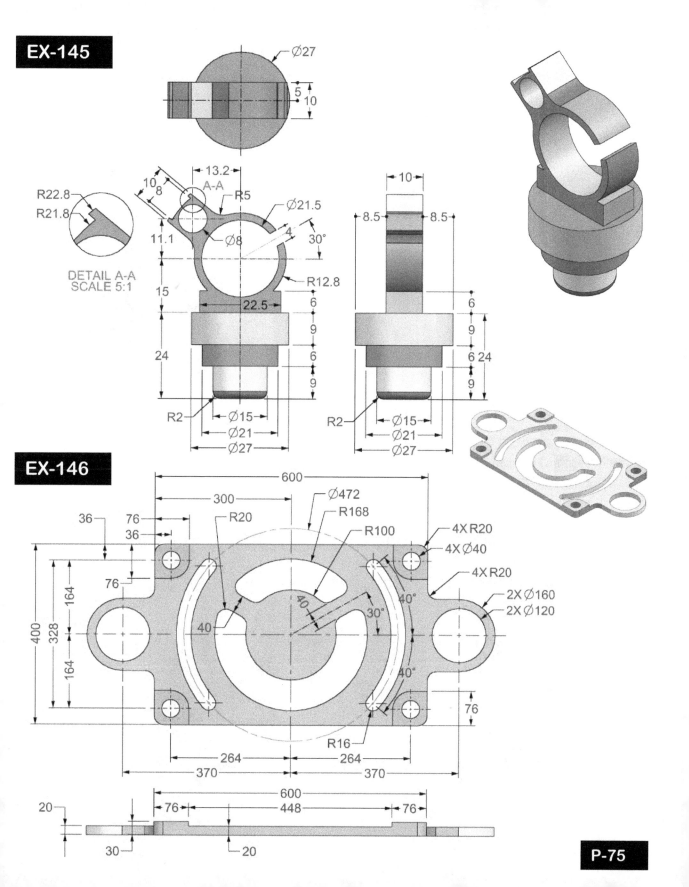

EX-145

Ø27

5
10

13.2
A-A
10
8
R5
Ø21.5
11.1
Ø8
4
30°
R22.8
R21.8
DETAIL A-A
SCALE 5:1
15
22.5
R12.8

10
8.5   8.5

6
9
6
9

6
9
6 24

24

R2   Ø15
Ø21
Ø27

R2   Ø15
Ø21
Ø27

EX-146

600
300
Ø472
R20
R168
R100
4X R20
4X Ø40
4X R20
36
76
36
76
164
328
400
164
40
40
40°
30°
40°
2X Ø160
2X Ø120
76
R16
264   264
370   370

600
76   448   76
20
30   20

P-75

Ø40
120°
Ø20
120°
10
60

R10

Ø40

200

79.6

Ø20
15
R15
60

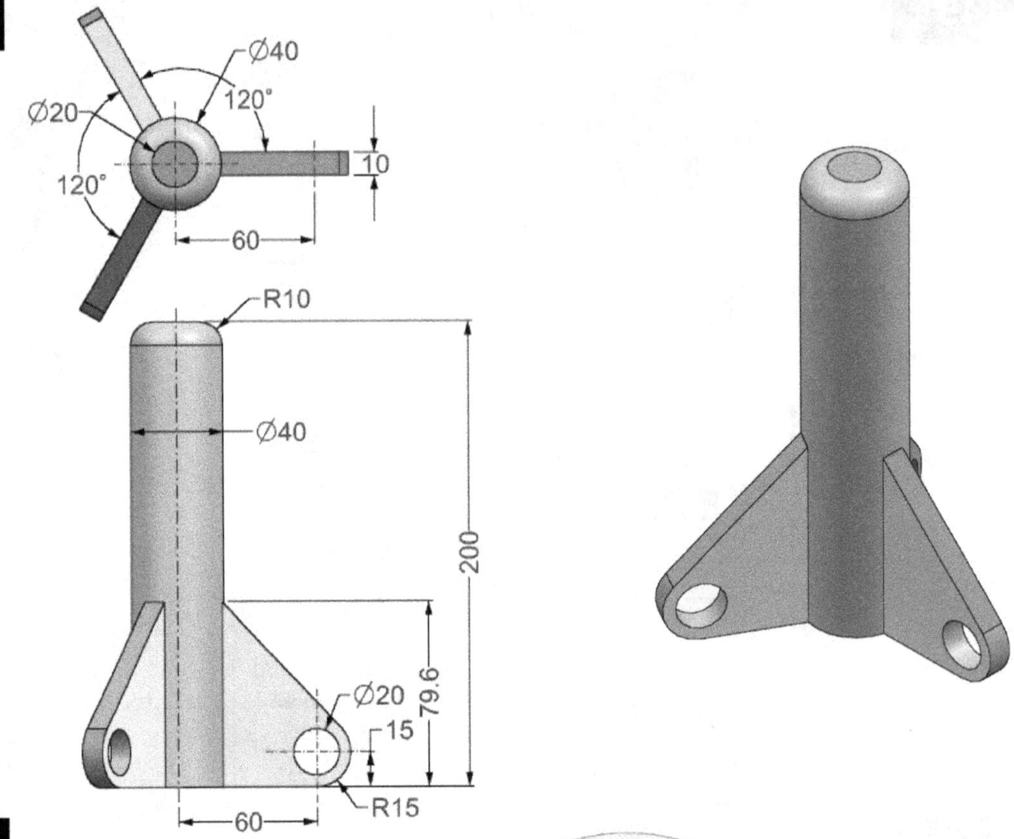

2X Ø100
2X Ø80
Ø50
R45
51.6
R40
Ø30
100
100

A
A

Ø90
Ø50
10
10
40
15
100
100

Ø80
Ø90
Ø80
Ø50
Ø30
10
Ø80
15
10
40
15
100
100

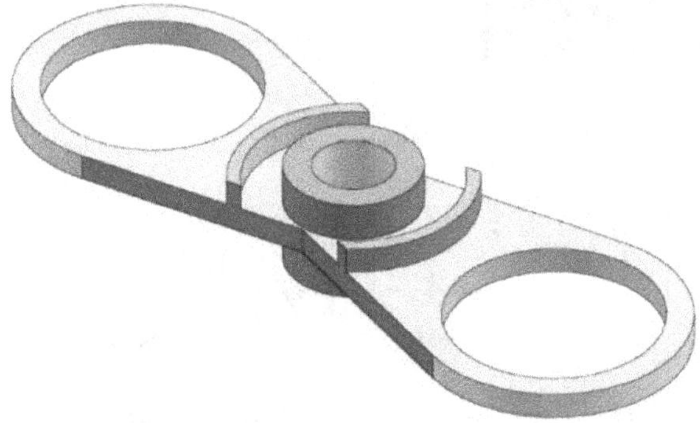

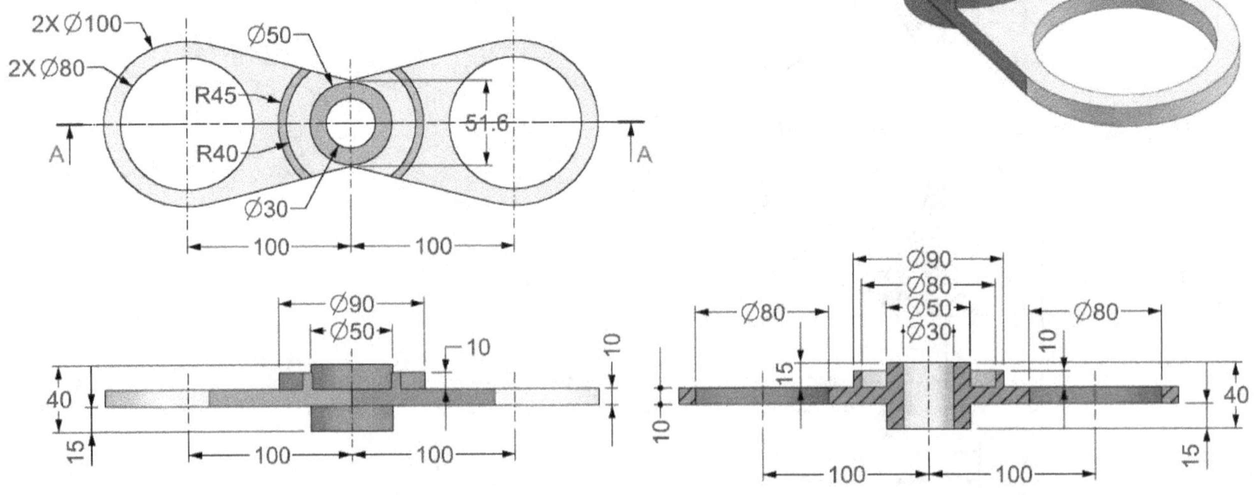

SECTION A-A

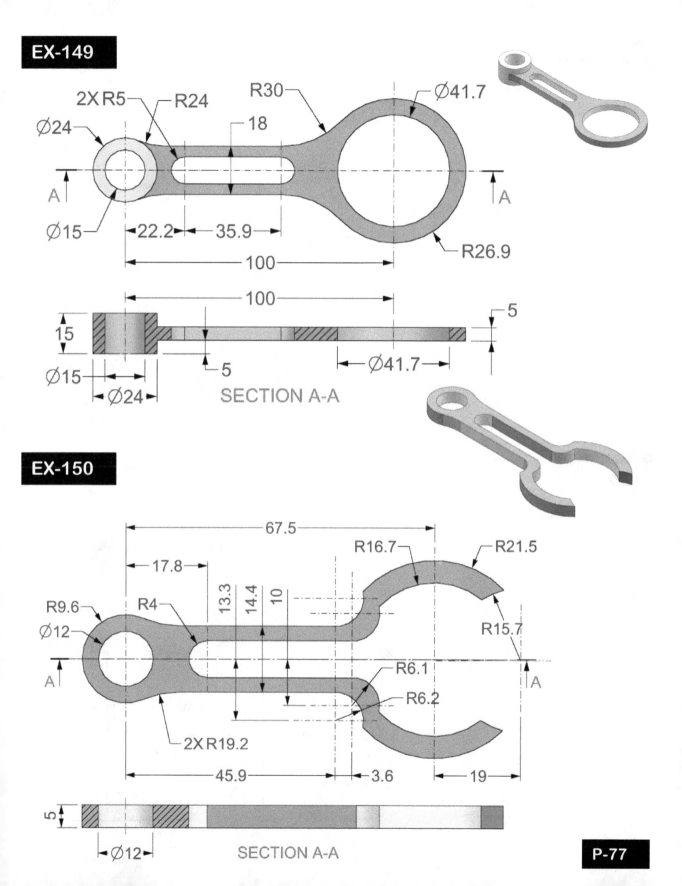

EX-149

2X R5 — R24

R30

Ø41.7

Ø24

18

R26.9

Ø15

22.2 35.9

100

100

15

5

Ø15

5

Ø24

Ø41.7

SECTION A-A

EX-150

67.5

17.8

R16.7

R21.5

R9.6

R4

13.3 14.4 10

R15.7

Ø12

R6.1

R6.2

2X R19.2

45.9

3.6

19

5

Ø12

SECTION A-A

P-77

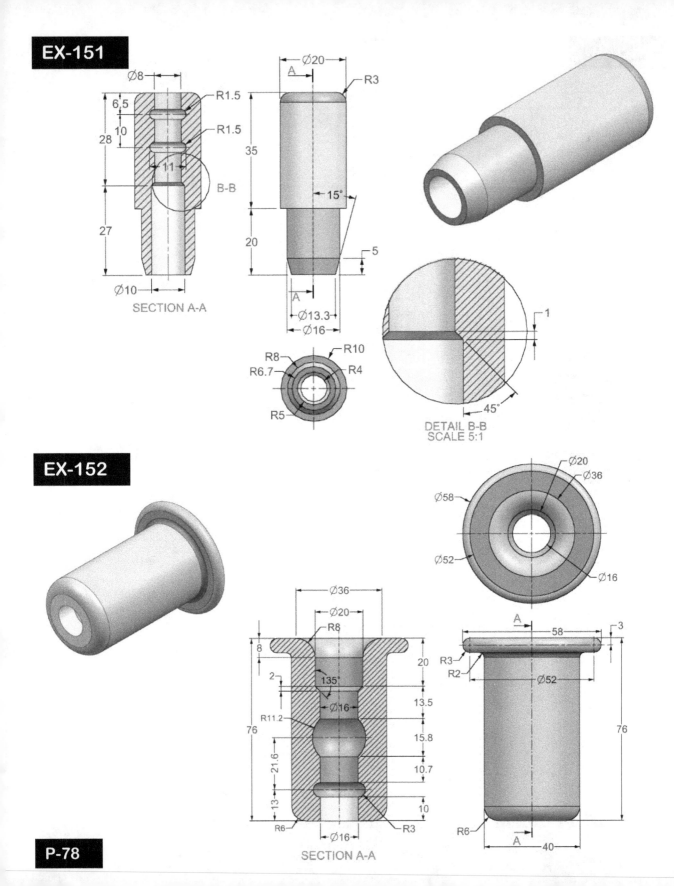

EX-151

Ø8

6.5
10
28

R1.5

R1.5

1 1

B-B

27

Ø10

SECTION A-A

Ø20

A

R3

35

15°

20

5

A

Ø13.3

Ø16

R8
R6.7
R10
R4

R5

1

45°

DETAIL B-B
SCALE 5:1

EX-152

Ø20
Ø36

Ø58

Ø52

Ø16

Ø36

Ø20

R8

8

A

58

3

20

R3
R2

2

135°

Ø16

Ø52

R11.2

13.5

76

15.8

76

21.6

10.7

13

10

R6

Ø16

R3

R6

A

40

SECTION A-A

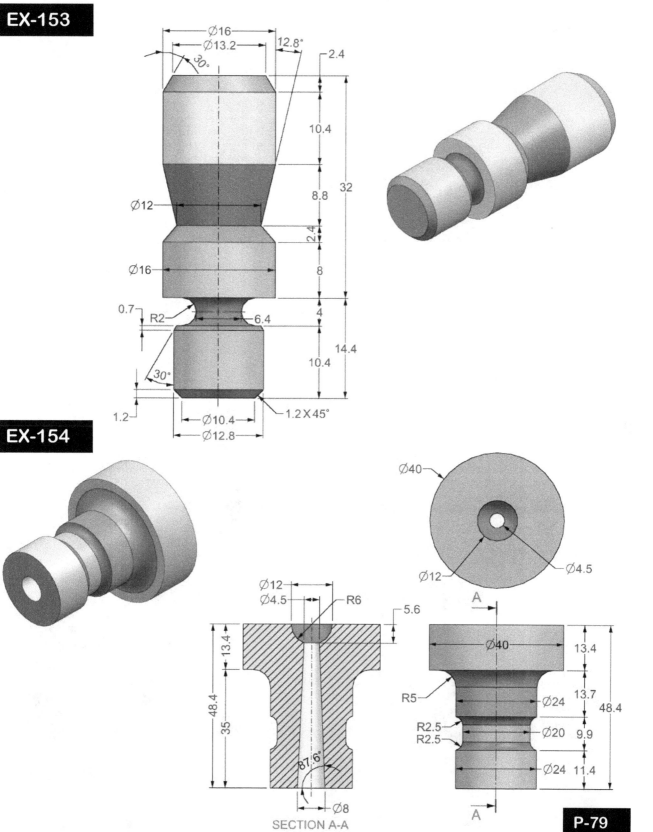

EX-153

Ø16
Ø13.2
12.8°
2.4
30°
10.4
32
8.8
Ø12
2.4
Ø16
8
0.7
R2
6.4
4
14.4
30°
10.4
1.2
Ø10.4
1.2 X 45°
Ø12.8

EX-154

Ø40
Ø12
Ø4.5
A

Ø12
Ø4.5
R6
5.6
48.4
13.4
35
87.6°
Ø8
SECTION A-A

Ø40
13.4
R5
13.7
Ø24
R2.5
R2.5
Ø20
48.4
9.9
Ø24
11.4
A

P-79

EX-155

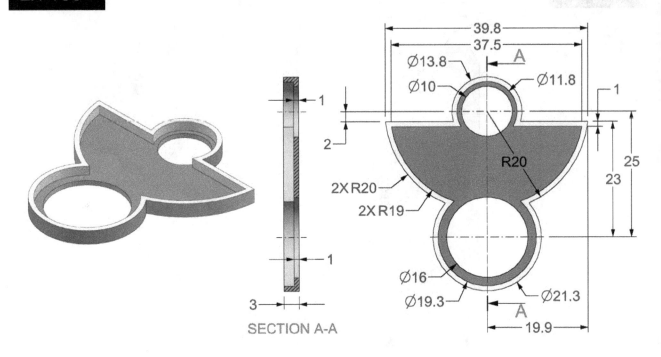

SECTION A-A

EX-156

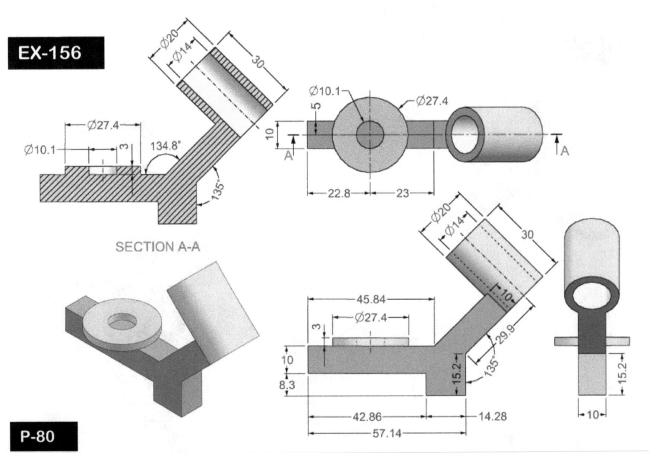

SECTION A-A

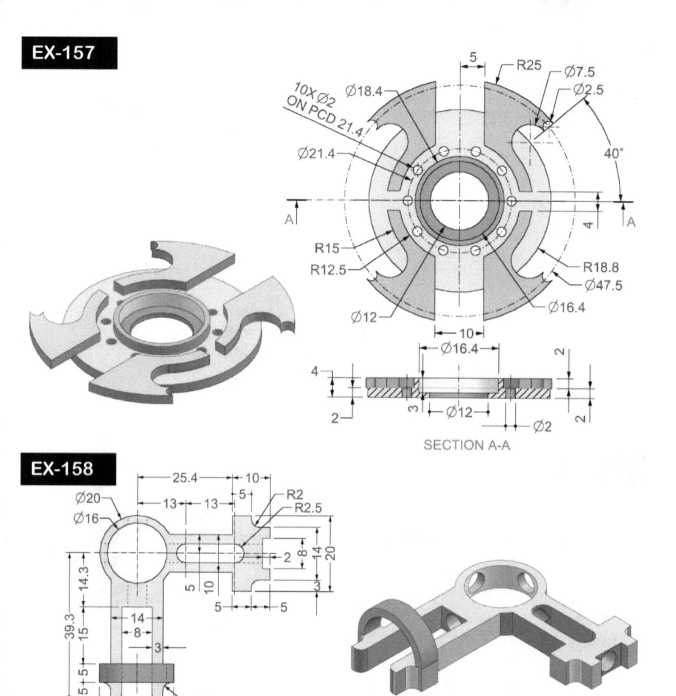

EX-157

10X Ø2
ON PCD 21.4
Ø18.4
5
R25
Ø7.5
Ø2.5
Ø21.4
40°
A
4
A
R15
R12.5
R18.8
Ø47.5
Ø12
Ø16.4
10
Ø16.4
2
4
3
Ø12
Ø2
2
2

SECTION A-A

EX-158

Ø20
Ø16
25.4
10
13
13
5
R2
R2.5
14.3
2
8
14
20
5
10
3
39.3
14
15
8
3
5
5
5
5
5
R2
R2
14
Ø20

Ø16
Ø20
Ø5
10
3
10
35.4
+5+5+

5
5
20
14
7
Ø5
6
6
3
6
39.3
10

P-81

EX-159

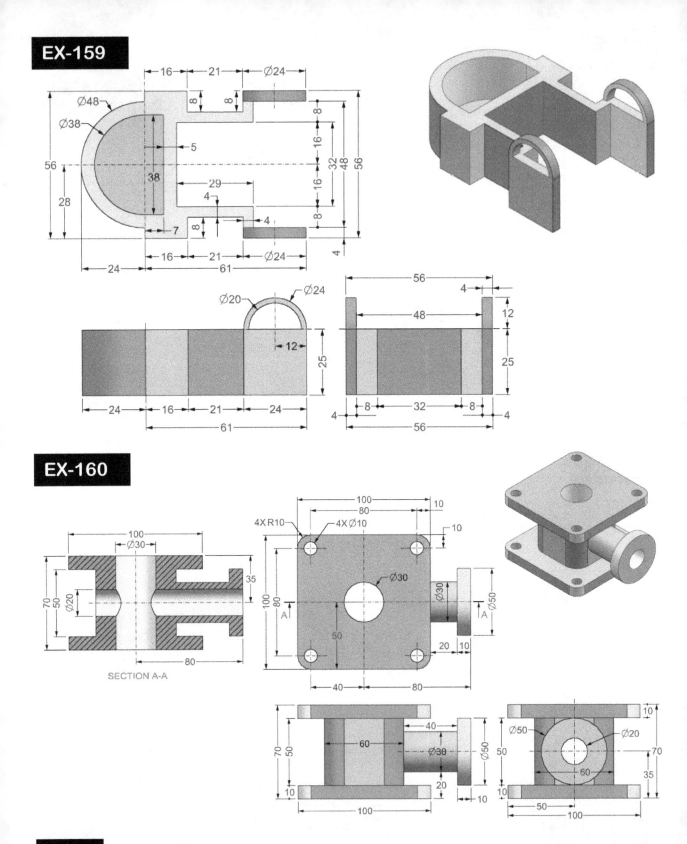

EX-160

SECTION A-A

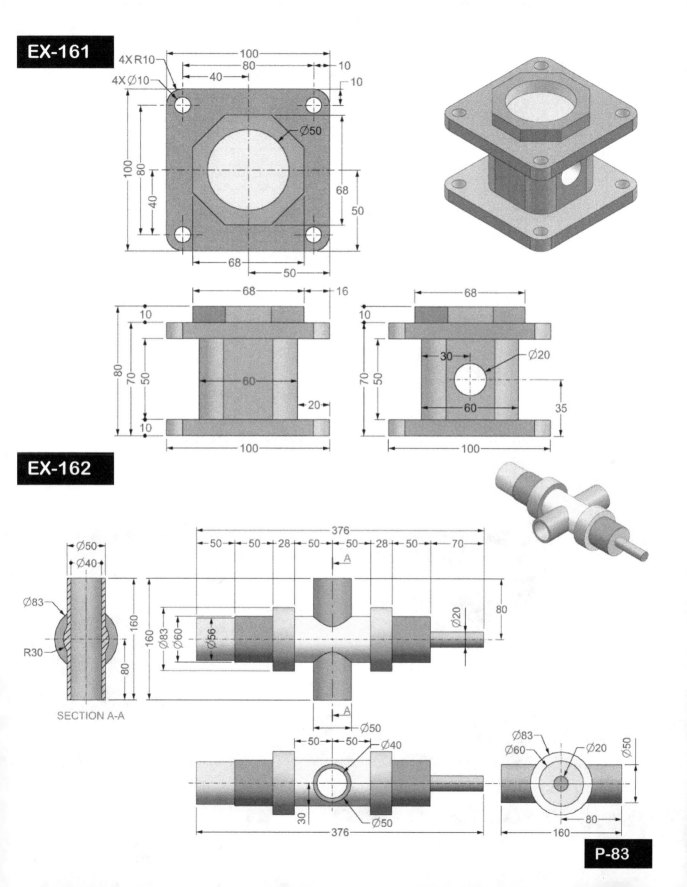

EX-161

4X R10
4X Ø10
100
80
40
10
10
100
80
40
Ø50
68
50
68
50

68
16
10
80
70
50
60
20
10
100

68
10
70
50
30
Ø20
60
35
100

EX-162

Ø50
Ø40
Ø83
R30
SECTION A-A

376
50 50 28 50 50 28 50 70
A
160
160
80
Ø83
Ø60
Ø56
Ø20
80
A

Ø50
50 50 Ø40
30
Ø50
376

Ø83
Ø60
Ø20
Ø50
80
160

P-83

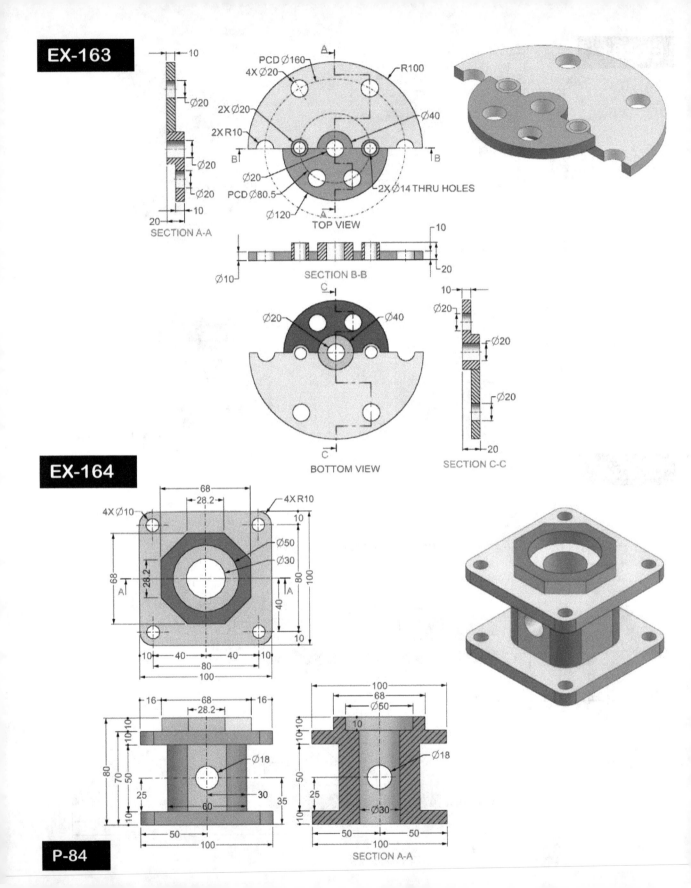

EX-163

10

Ø20

Ø20

Ø20

10

20

SECTION A-A

A

PCD Ø160
4X Ø20
R100
2X Ø20
2X R10
Ø40
Ø20
2X Ø14 THRU HOLES
PCD Ø80.5
Ø120
B B
A

TOP VIEW

Ø10

10
20

SECTION B-B

C

Ø20
Ø40
Ø20

C

BOTTOM VIEW

10
Ø20
Ø20
Ø20
20

SECTION C-C

EX-164

68
28.2
4X R10
4X Ø10
10
Ø50
Ø30
68
28.2
80
100
A A
40
10
10
40
40
10
80
100

16
68
16
10 10
28.2
80
70
50
25
Ø18
10
30
60
50
100

100
68
Ø50
10
10 10
50
Ø18
25
10
35
Ø30
50
50
100

SECTION A-A

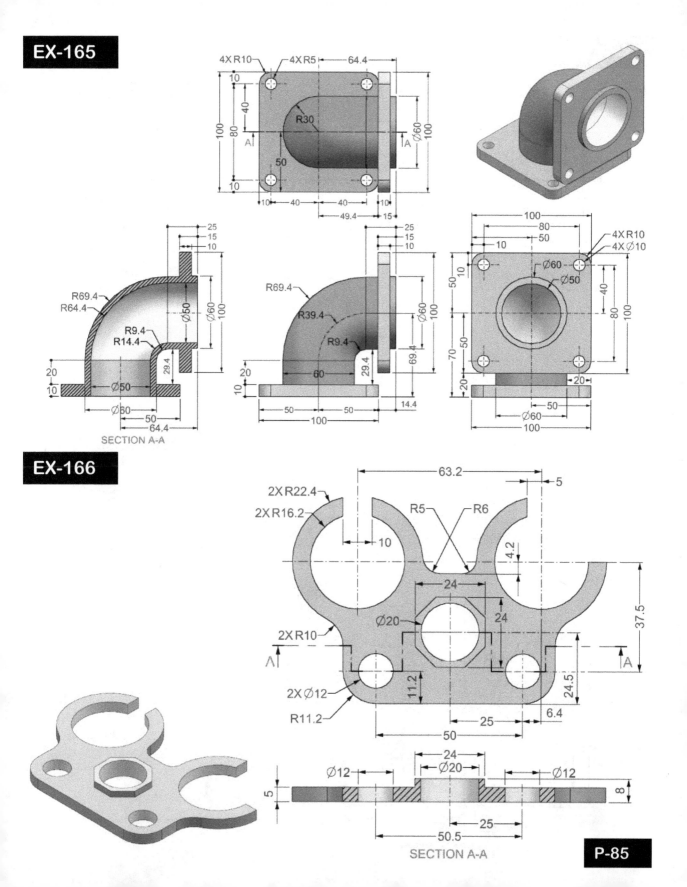

EX-165

4X R10   4X R5   64.4
10
40
80
R30
100
Ø60
100
A   A
50
10
10   40   40   10
49.4   15

25
15
10
R69.4
R64.4
Ø50
Ø60
100
R9.4
R14.4
29.4
20
10
Ø50
Ø60
50
64.4
SECTION A-A

25
15
10
R69.4
Ø60
100
R39.4
69.4
R9.4
29.4
20
10
60
14.4
50   50
100

100
80
50
10
4X R10
4X Ø10
Ø60
Ø50
50
40
10
80
100
50
70
20
20
50
Ø60
100

EX-166

63.2   5
2X R22.4
2X R16.2
R5   R6
10
4.2
24
Ø20
24
2X R10
A   A
37.5
2X Ø12
11.2
24.5
R11.2
6.4
25
50

24
Ø20
Ø12   Ø12
5
8
25
50.5
SECTION A-A

P-85

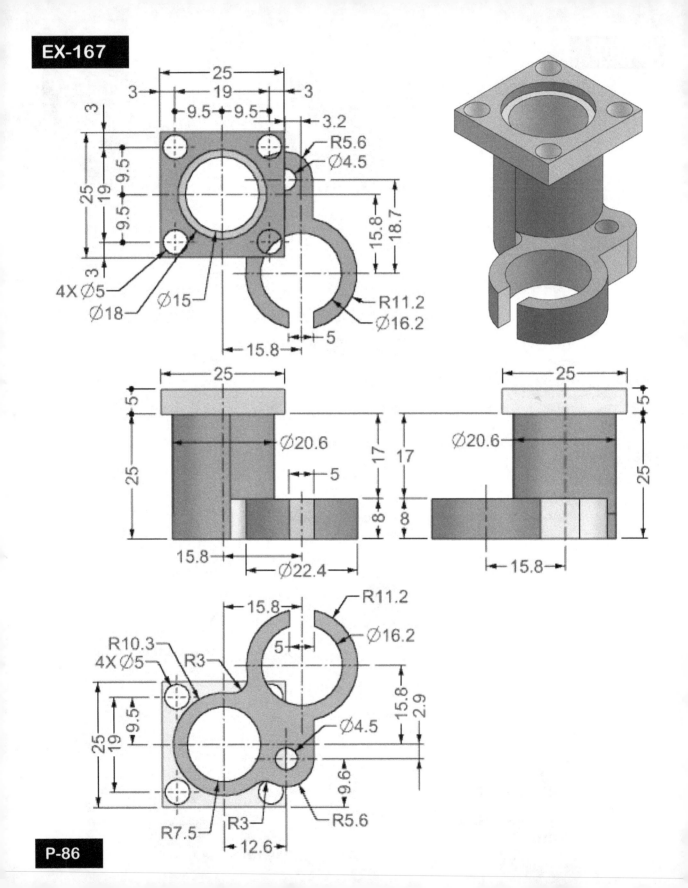

EX-168

Ø120
PCD Ø95
8X Ø14
8X Ø10 ON PCD 95
R35
R25
6
3
A — A

30
32
80 16
32
20
2
Ø70
Ø120

30
Ø14
Ø10
16 20
Ø50
Ø70
PCD 95
Ø120

SECTION A-A

EX-169

Ø70
Ø40
20
40
R5
Ø28
Ø40
50
130
70
200

Ø70
R2
R60
Ø80
R5
30
40
140
21.3
80
50
Ø28
Ø40
30
10
50
80
70

Ø70
15 — 40 — 15
10
30
Ø28
Ø40
80
15
15
70
30
10
35
Ø70

P-87

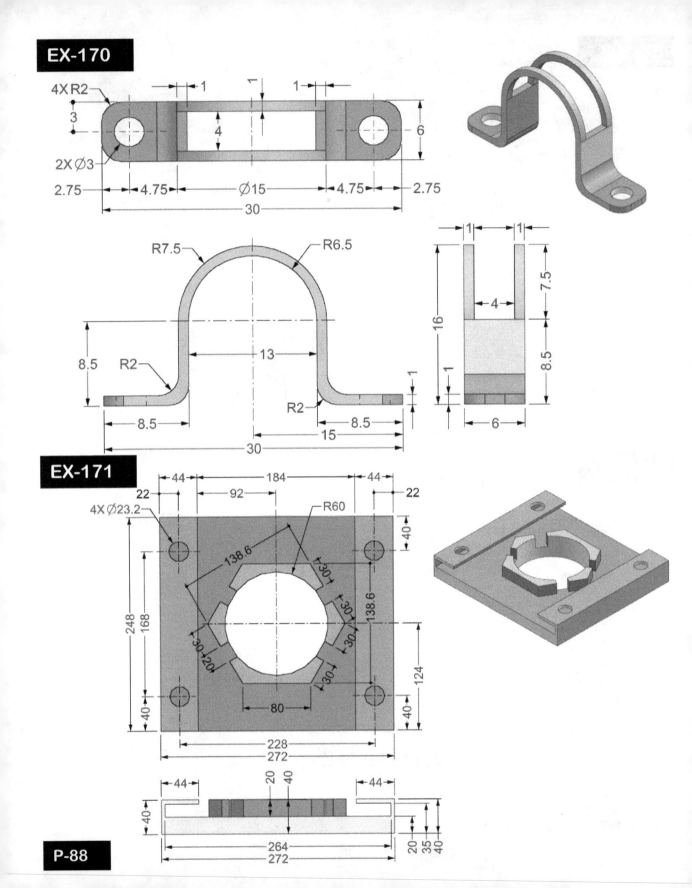

EX-170

4X R2
3
2X Ø3
2.75 — 4.75 — Ø15 — 4.75 — 2.75
30
1 — 1 — 1
4
6

R7.5 — R6.5
R2
8.5
13
R2
8.5 — 8.5
15
30

1 — 1
7.5
16 — 4
8.5
1 — 1
6

EX-171

44 — 184 — 44
22 — 92 — 22
4X Ø23.2
R60
138.6
30
30
30
248 — 168 — 138.6
30 — 20
30
124
80
40
228
272

44 — 20 — 40 — 44
40 — 20
264 — 35
272 — 40

P-88

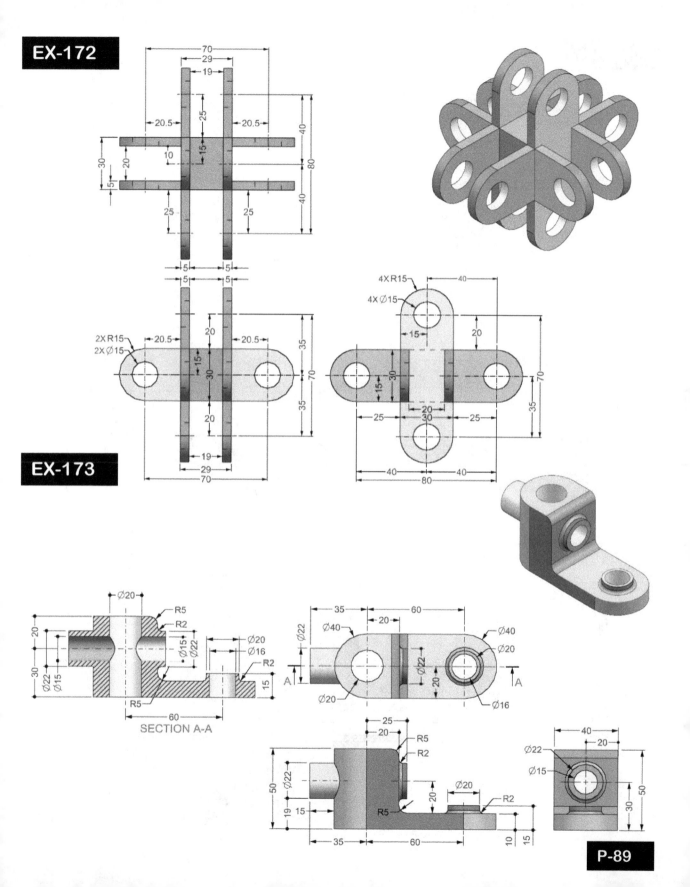

EX-172

EX-173

2X R15
2X Ø15

4X R15
4X Ø15

SECTION A-A

P-89

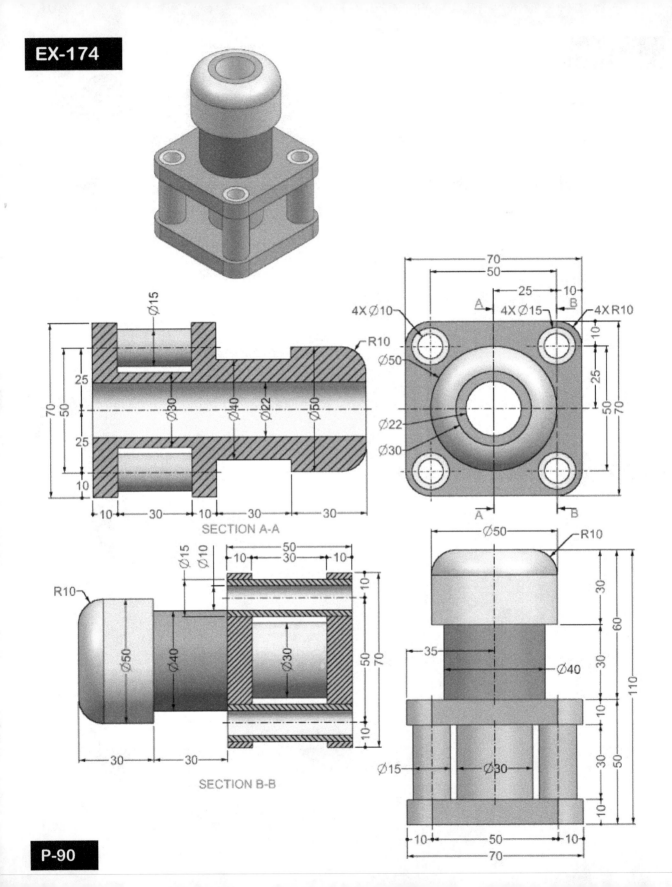

EX-174

SECTION A-A

SECTION B-B

P-90

4X Ø15
4X Ø10
Ø30
Ø22
4X R10
70
35 35
10 25 25 10
10
35
25
70
25
35
10
A A

Ø30
Ø15 Ø15
Ø15 Ø15
50
70
20
5
10
30
50
10

Ø30
Ø22
Ø15
Ø10
20
30
5
10
70
30
10
Ø22
25 25
50
70

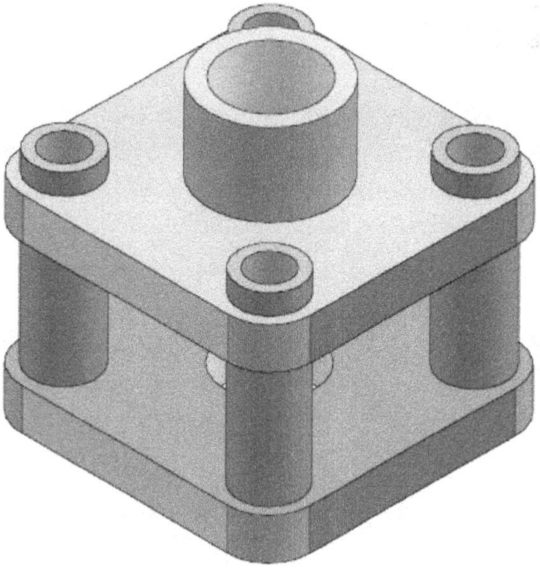

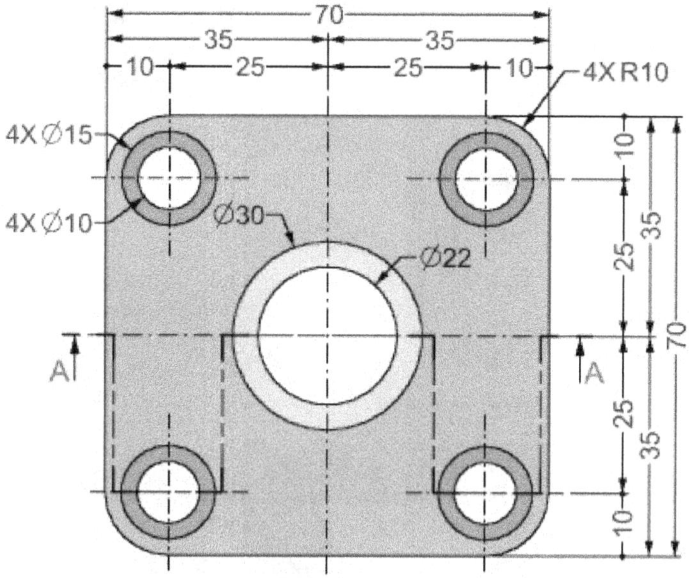

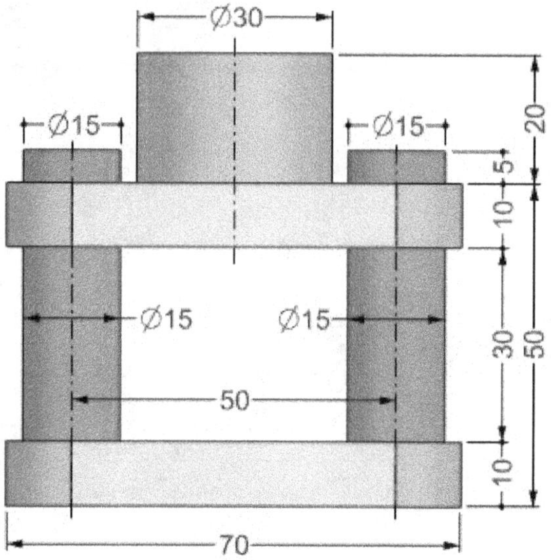

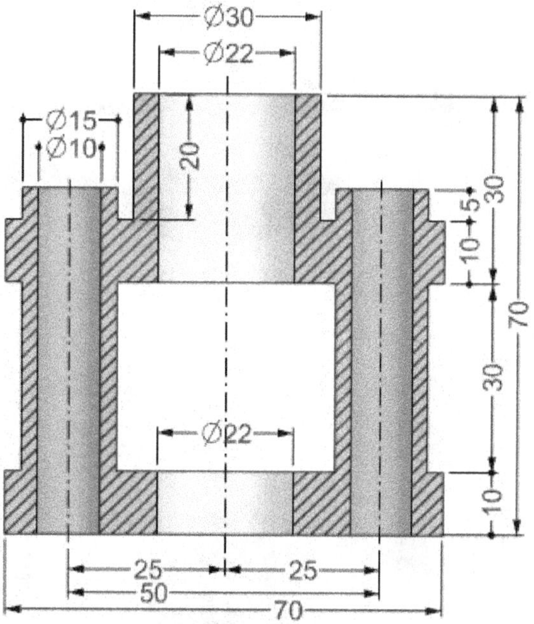

SECTION A-A

EX-176

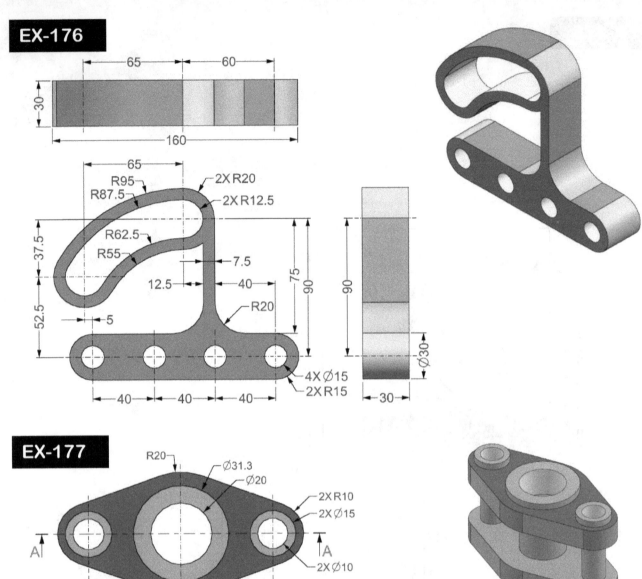

EX-177

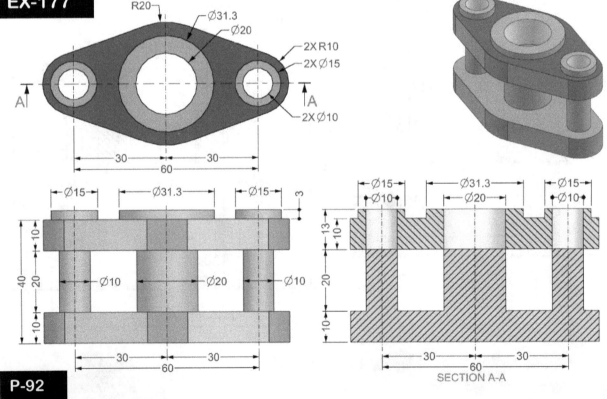

SECTION A-A

P-92

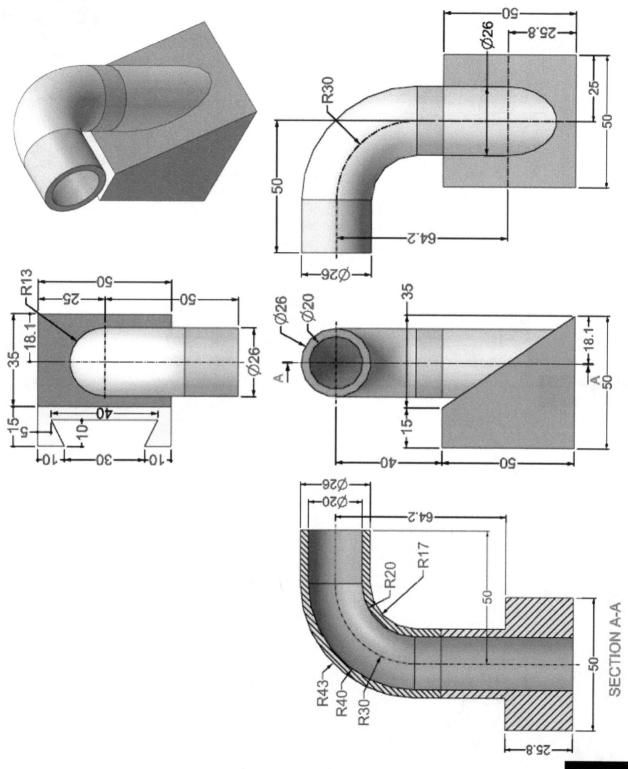

R30

Ø26

50

25.8

25

50

64.2

Ø26

R13

50

25

50

35

18.1

Ø26

40

10

15

5

10

30

10

Ø26

Ø20

35

18.1

50

15

40

50

A

A

Ø26

Ø20

64.2

R20

R17

50

R43

R40

R30

50

25.8

SECTION A-A

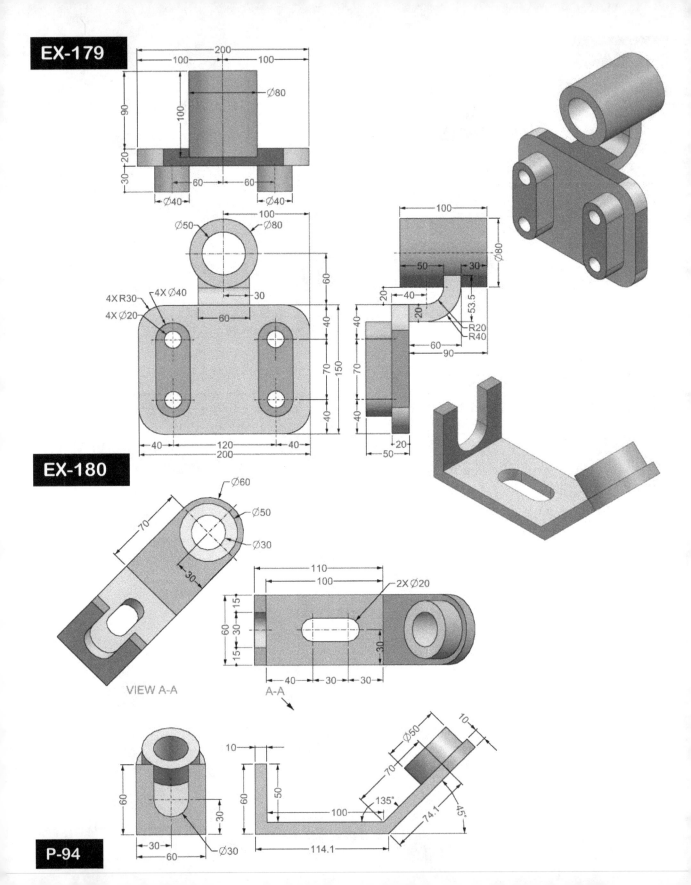

EX-179

EX-180

VIEW A-A

A-A

P-94

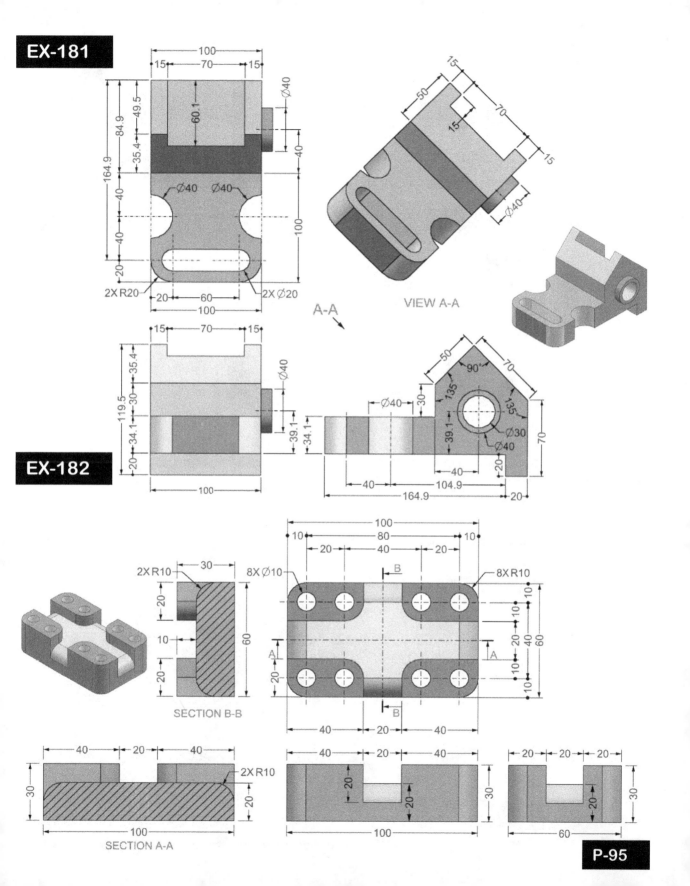

EX-181

Ø40
100
70
15
60.1
49.5
84.9
35.4
164.9
40
Ø40   Ø40
40
40
100
20
2X R20
20
60
100
2X Ø20

VIEW A-A

A-A

15
50
70
15
15
Ø40

EX-182

15   70   15
35.4
119.5
30
Ø40
34.1
39.1
20
100

Ø40
50
70
90°
135
135
30
39.1
Ø30
Ø40
34.1
20
40
40
104.9
20
164.9

2X R10
30
20
10
60
20
SECTION B-B

100
80
10
20   40   20
10
8X Ø10
B
10
10
20
40
60
8X R10
A
A
20
10
B
40   20   40

40   20   40
30
20
2X R10
100
SECTION A-A

40   20   40
20   20
30
100

20   20   20
20
30
60

P-95

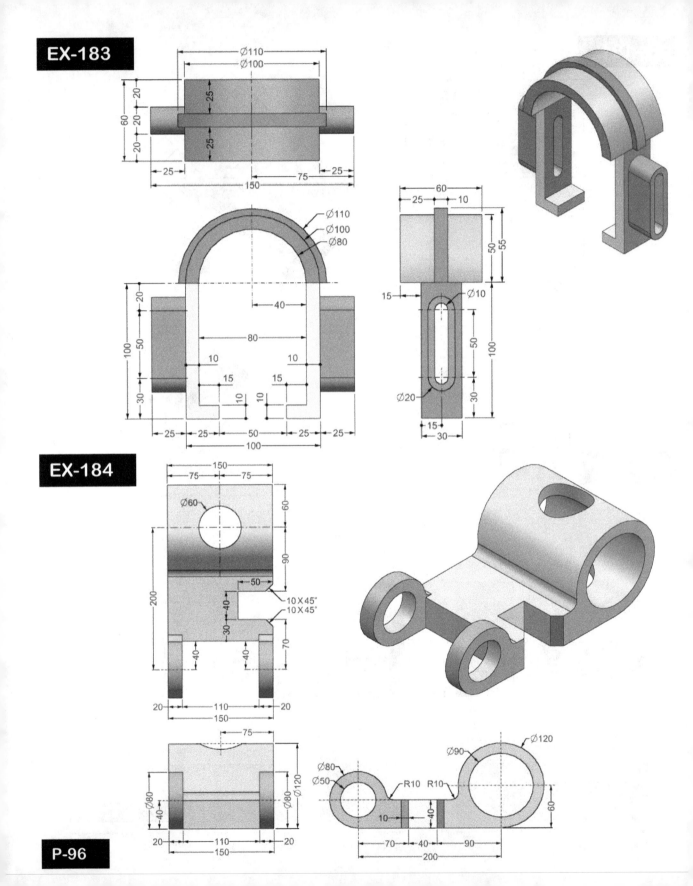

EX-183

Ø110
Ø100
20
20
20
60
25
25
25
75
25
150

Ø110
Ø100
Ø80
20
100
50
40
80
30
10   10
15   15
10 10
25 25 50 25 25
100

60
25   10
50
55
15
Ø10
50
100
Ø20
15
30

EX-184

150
75   75
Ø60
60
90
200
50
40
10 X 45°
30
10 X 45°
70
40   40
20   110   20
150

75
Ø80
Ø120
Ø80
40
20   110   20
150

Ø90   Ø120
Ø80
Ø50
R10   R10
10
40
60
70   40   90
200

P-96

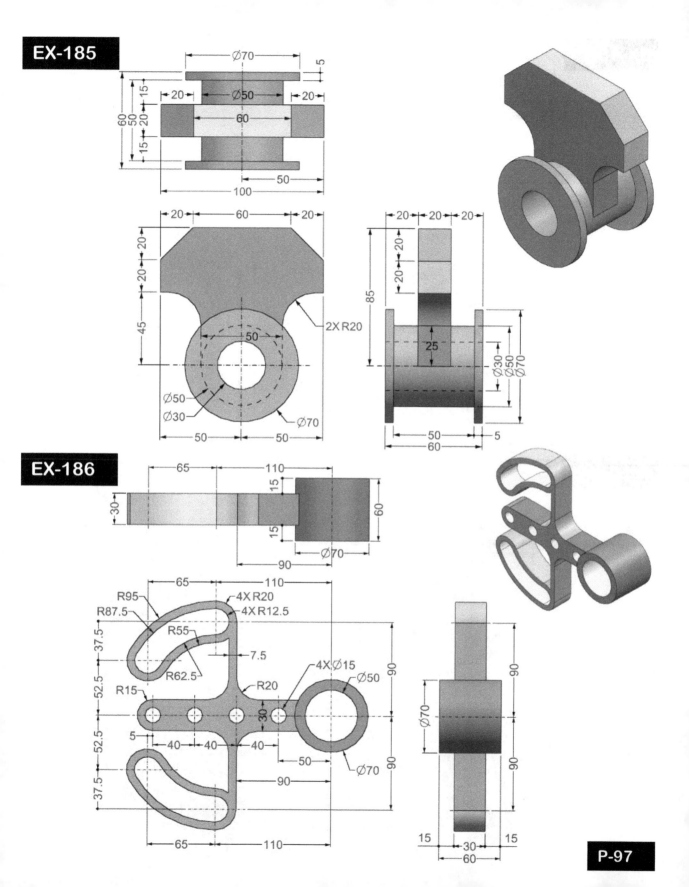

EX-185

Ø70
5
15
20
60
50
20
15
20
Ø50
60
20
50
100

20
60
20
20
20
45
50
2X R20
Ø50
Ø30
Ø70
50
50

20
20
20
20
20
85
25
Ø30
Ø50
Ø70
50
5
60

EX-186

65
110
15
30
15
60
90
Ø70

65
110
R95
4X R20
R87.5
4X R12.5
37.5
R55
7.5
52.5
R62.5
4X Ø15
R15
R20
Ø50
30
52.5
5
40
40
40
50
37.5
90
Ø70
65
110

90
Ø70
90
15
30
15
60

P-97

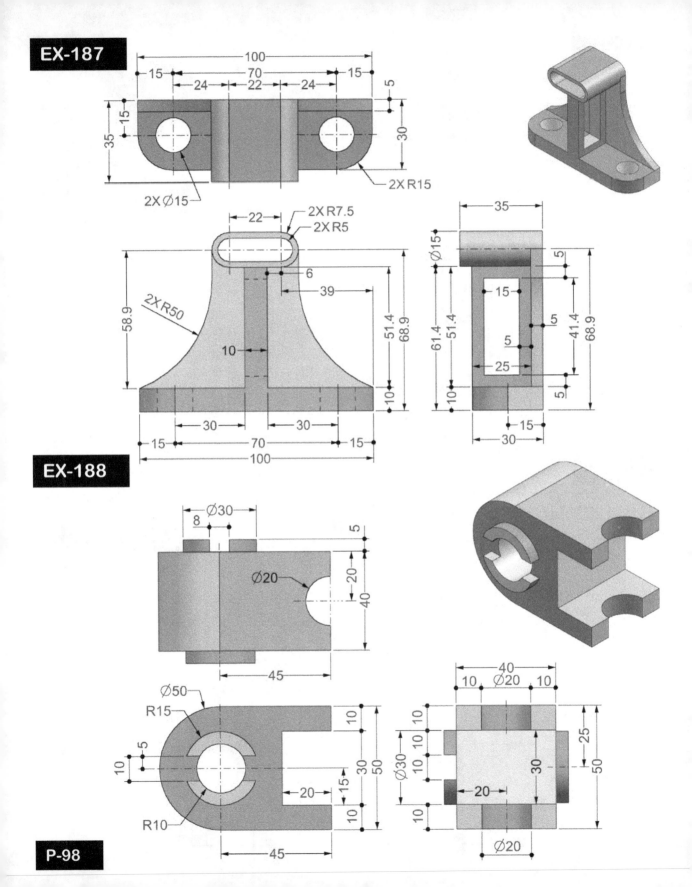

EX-187

2X∅15
2X R15
2X R7.5
2X R5
6
39
2X R50
10
∅15

EX-188

∅30
8
∅20
45
∅50
R15
R10
20
∅30
∅20
40
∅20
20
∅20

P-98

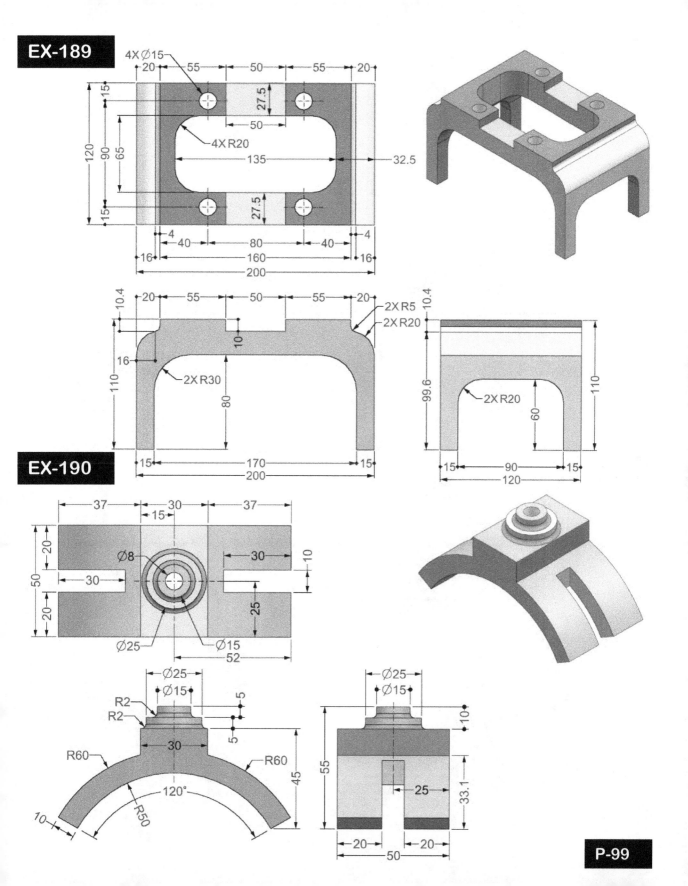

EX-189

4X Ø15
20 — 55 — 50 — 55 — 20
15
120
90
65
27.5
50
4X R20
135 — 32.5
27.5
15
4
40 — 80 — 40
16 — 160 — 16
200

10.4
20 — 55 — 50 — 55 — 20
2X R5
2X R20
16
110
80
10
2X R30
15 — 170 — 15
200

10.4
99.6
110
2X R20
60
15 — 90 — 15
120

EX-190

37 — 30 — 37
15
20
50
20
Ø8
30
30
10
25
Ø25 — Ø15
52

Ø25
Ø15
R2
R2
5
30
5
R60
R60
120°
45
R50
10

Ø25
Ø15
10
55
33.1
25
20 — 20
50

P-99

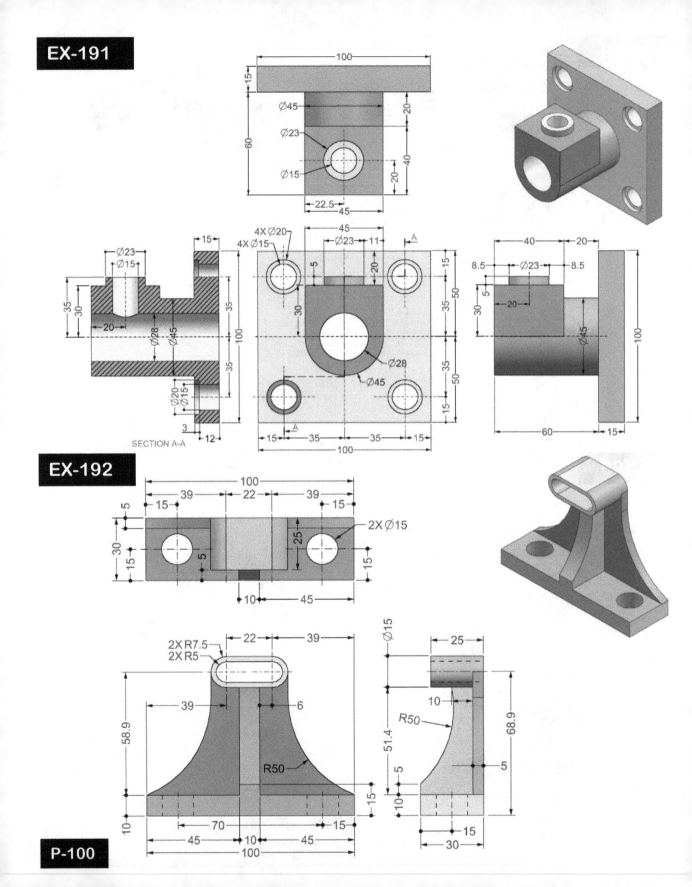

EX-191

SECTION A-A

EX-192

P-100

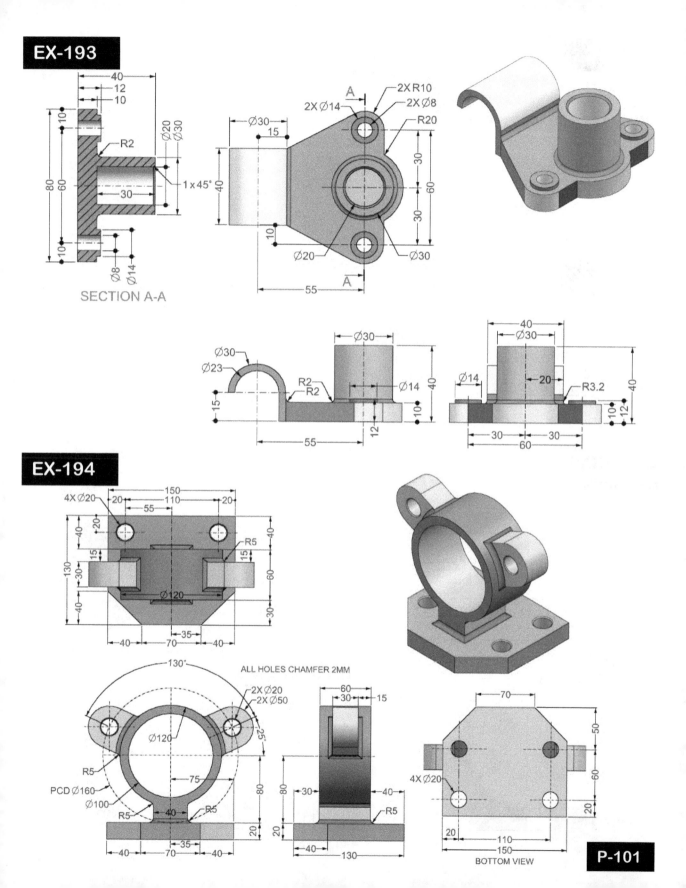

EX-193

SECTION A-A

2X R10
2X Ø8
2X Ø14
R20
Ø30
15
Ø30
40
Ø20
55
Ø30

40
12
10
R2
Ø20
Ø30
80
60
R2
30
1 x 45°
10
10
Ø8
Ø14

Ø30
Ø23
R2
R2
15
55
Ø30
Ø14
40
10
12

40
Ø30
Ø14
20
R3.2
40
10
12
30
30
60

EX-194

4X Ø20
20
150
110
20
55
20
40
R5
40
15
15
130
30
60
Ø120
40
30
40
70
40
35

130°
ALL HOLES CHAMFER 2MM
2X Ø20
2X Ø50
Ø120
25
R5
75
PCD Ø160
Ø100
80
R5
40
R5
20
40
70
40
35

60
30
15
80
30
40
20
R5
40
130

70
50
60
4X Ø20
20
20
110
150
BOTTOM VIEW

P-101

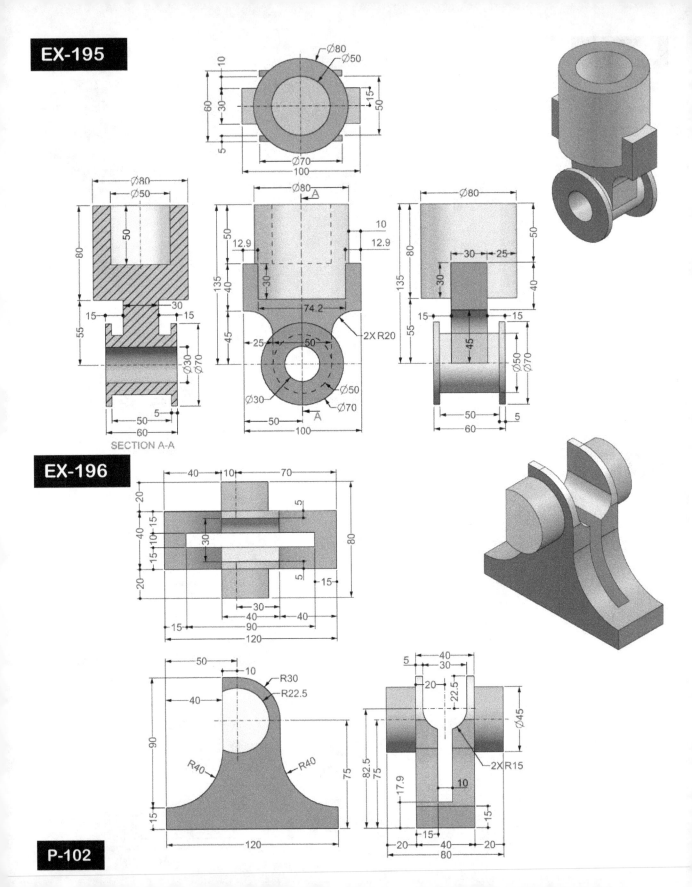

EX-195

∅80
∅50
10
60
30
50
15
5
∅70
100

∅80
∅50
50
80
15
15
30
55
∅30
∅70
50
5
60
SECTION A-A

∅80
A
50
12.9
10
12.9
135
40
30
74.2
2X R20
45
25
50
∅30
50
∅50
∅70
A
100

∅80
80
30
25
30
40
135
15
45
15
55
∅50
∅70
50
5
60

EX-196

40
10
70
20
5
40
15
10
15
30
80
15
5
20
15
30
40
40
15
90
120

50
10
R30
R22.5
40
90
R40
R40
75
15
120

5
40
30
20
22.5
∅45
82.5
75
2X R15
17.9
10
15
15
20
40
20
80

P-102

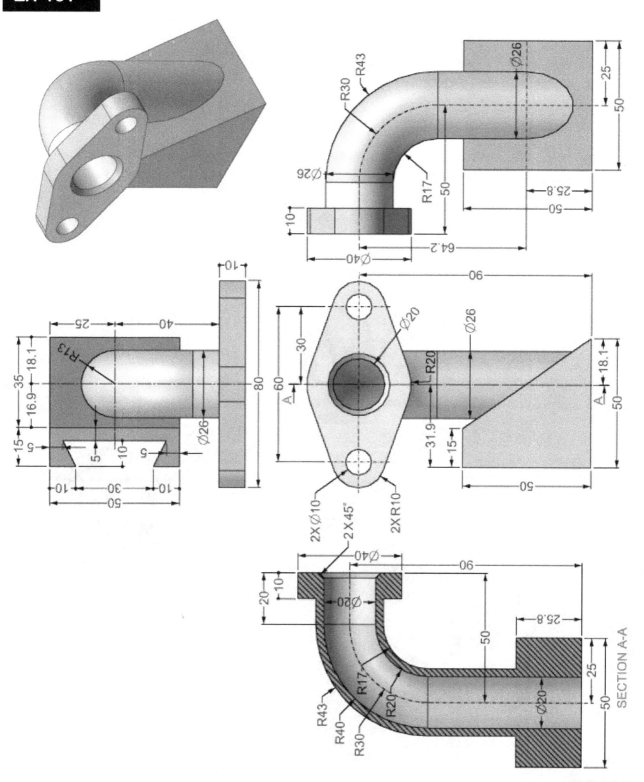

R30
R43
Ø26
25
50
Ø26
25.8
50
R17
50
10
64.2
Ø40

10
25
40
R13
35
18.1
16.9
15
5
5
10
5
Ø26
80
10
30
10
50

60
30
A
Ø20
90
Ø26
R20
A
18.1
31.9
15
50
50

2X Ø10
2 X 45°
2X R10

40
Ø40
20
10
Ø20
90
R17
50
R20
R43
25.8
R40
25
R30
Ø20
50

SECTION A-A

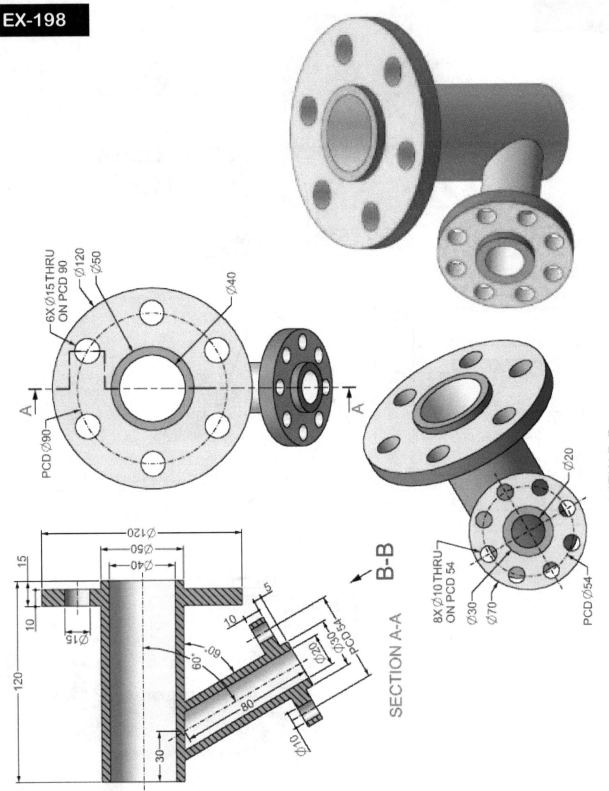

6X Ø15THRU ON PCD 90
Ø120
Ø50
Ø40
PCD Ø90

VIEW B-B

Ø20
8X Ø10THRU ON PCD 54
Ø30
Ø70
PCD 54

B-B

SECTION A-A

Ø120
Ø50
Ø40
15
10
Ø15
120
30
5
10
60°
60°
80
Ø30
Ø20
PCD 54
Ø10

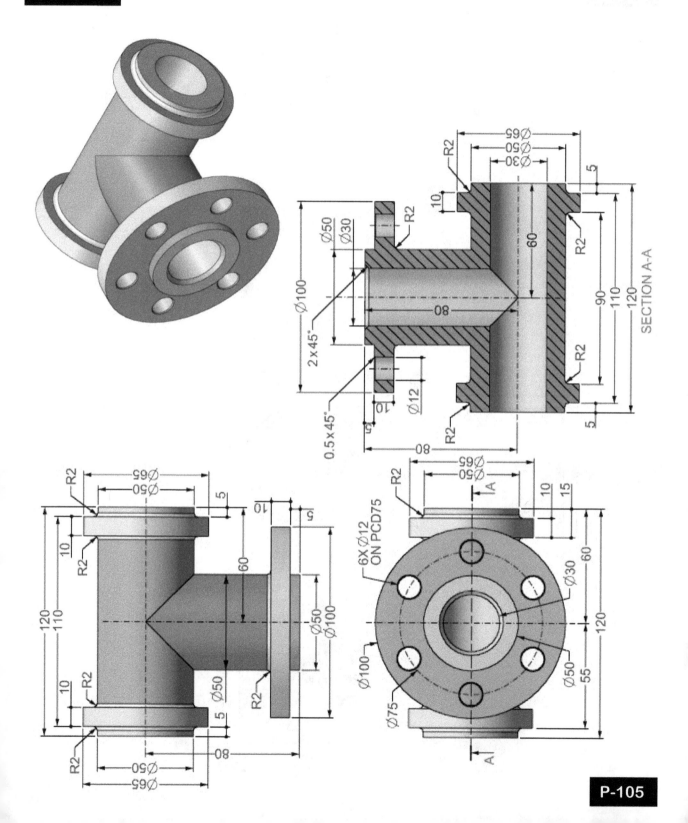

SECTION A-A

6X Ø12
ON PCD75

SECTION C-C

Ø90
Ø76
Ø86
Ø34
D-D

DETAIL D-D
SCALE 2:1

Ø24
12
10
Ø20

Thickness 2 mm
All sides

2X R10

20
60
22
45
C
C
B
B
Ø80
Ø90

12
33
80
84
Ø34
2
3X45°
17
Ø30

SECTION B-B

R5
Ø90
Ø80
102
2

Ø90
Ø30
A
A
Ø80
3X45°

R5
R3
3X45°
Ø80
Ø76
17
Ø30
Ø84
102
Ø86
Ø90

Thickness 2 mm
All sides

SECTION A-A

Other useful books by CADIN360

1. 150 CAD Exercises

2. AutoCAD Exercises

3. CAD Exercises

4. 50+ SolidWorks Exercises

5. SolidWorks 200 Exercises

6. Autodesk Inventor Exercises

7. Catia Exercises

8. Siemens NX Exercises